BITING THE BULLET

BITING THE BULLET

Some Personal Reflections on Religious Education

Chris Arthur

THE SAINT ANDREW PRESS
EDINBURGH

First published in 1990 by
THE SAINT ANDREW PRESS
121 George Street, Edinburgh EH2 4YN

Copyright © Chris Arthur 1990

ISBN 0 7152 0635 4

British Library Cataloguing in Publication Data
Arthur, Chris
Biting the bullet: some personal reflections on religious
education.
1. Schools. Religious education
I. Title
200'.7

ISBN 0-7152-0635-4

This book is set in 10/11pt Times.

Typeset by Bookworm Typesetting Ltd, Edinburgh.
**Printed in Great Britain by
Billing & Sons Ltd, Worcester**

Cover photograph: Ewen Weatherspoon

Contents

'We have just enough religion to make us hate,
but not enough to make us love, one another.'
Jonathan Swift

This book is dedicated to those who work against
religious hatred, wherever it occurs.

The author's royalties from the sale of this volume have
been donated to

ALL CHILDREN TOGETHER

ALL CHILDREN TOGETHER exists to support integrated
education by consent in Northern Ireland. Several integrated
schools, where Protestant and Catholic children may learn
together, have been set up already and more are planned. **ALL
CHILDREN TOGETHER** is a registered charity.
All donations, however small, are welcome.

Readers wishing to make a donation, or to know more about the
work of this organization, should write to:
ALL CHILDREN TOGETHER, 13 University Street, Belfast
BT7 1FY, Northern Ireland.

*This donation of royalties simply indicates the author's support
for integrated education in Northern Ireland. It does not imply
that ALL CHILDREN TOGETHER agrees with the opinions
expressed in the pages which follow, or that religious education
in any integrated school is conducted along the lines
suggested here.*

Preface

Most of the constituent parts of this book started out as articles or lectures and were therefore intended to be *individually* intelligible. I hope that something of their self-contained nature survives here. Whilst I have tried to avoid the temptation of simply stringing together a series of unconnected articles, I have also tried not to let the 'character' of the individual pieces get lost in a book-length text. As I explain in the introduction, to the extent that it could be compared to visual art, this book is intended as a display of sketches, rather than a single, finished portrait. As such, I hope that readers will feel able to move from one view to another in the order they see fit, without feeling overly constrained by the serial imperative which chapters tend to impose.

My aim in writing this book will have been served if it causes even a few readers who had not done so before to see how important proper education in this neglected area is.

Chris Arthur
Edinburgh 1989

Introduction

If someone told me that the world was flat, that the moon was made of green cheese and that $2 + 2 = 5$, I would probably reach for one of three convenient explanations to account for their erroneous opinions. Either the person in question was mad, or they were indulging in a practical joke, or, somewhere along the line, something had gone terribly wrong with their education. When, as happened shortly after the Zeebrugge ferry disaster, I was handed a pamphlet which viewed it as 'God's message to the nation', the same three explanations suggested themselves. Surely anyone who sees such tragic loss of life as 'a chastening from the Lord' and uses it to expound a message in which 'the infidel spirit of evolution' is blamed for any panic which ensued when the Herald of Free Enterprise went down, must be mad, or engaged in some sick joke of momentously bad taste, or else be displaying all the symptoms of a massive educational failure.

The young man who handed me that particular tract did not appear obviously insane, nor did he seem anything but serious, so I conclude that he must have fallen victim to an educational deficiency so severe that it had caused blindness in that part of his mind's eye which dealt with religious matters. The writer of the tract and those involved with its street distribution must surely have been suffering from some sort of spiritual scurvy, occasioned by an absence of the right educational vitamins. Whatever teaching they had received at school must have made little impact, or else have offered a dangerously unhealthy diet when it came to dealing with human religiousness.

Although the 'Zeebrugge tract' may have been a particularly striking example of what a lack of proper religious education can lead to, it is far from being a unique or even particularly uncommon phenomenon. I can recall many other occasions when I have been approached by some sort of religious pamphleteer intent on 'saving me' by drawing some sort of spurious theological moral from current affairs. From the point of view of such tract writers, AIDS is (quite literally) a godsend and even the prospect of nuclear destruction can be pressed into service as part of God's plan for humankind.

The religious illiteracy which such tracts display is widespread and potentially as crippling for personal development as the illiteracy which stops someone from reading or writing. Despite this, adequate religious education in British schools remains disturbingly rare. The subject is given low priority in terms of time allocation, resources, and specialist staff. Many (if not most) pupils, parents and teachers continue to see it as an area of only marginal concern compared to other subjects.

It is comparatively easy to imagine what would happen if education failed in other areas. A society which did not attend to schooling in its language and literature would eventually produce an inarticulate populace; if mathematics was given insufficient emphasis, all manner of debilitating inaccuracies would gradually creep into every area of communication and commerce; if science was skimped on, things would stop being made—technology, medicine, manufacturing, all would be impaired.

Every area of ignorance bears its own particular cost which the individual, and the society to which they belong, must eventually pay. That the costs of *religious* ignorance are often horrendously and cripplingly high seems to be conveniently forgotten when it comes to making provision for education in this area. Would the intolerance, bigotry and hatred which has spawned murder, atrocity and destruction all across the world, from Belfast to Tehran, from Amritsar to Jerusalem, have happened if education had adequately extended its reach into the religious realm?

Whilst it may be more difficult to specify what would constitute adequate religious education than to lay down similar conditions for adequacy in other areas of learning, it is surely clear that most of what is printed in fundamentalist tracts is written from and addressed to a level of understanding about religious matters which is wholly unacceptable, and which would be regarded as educationally scandalous if it occurred in any other subject area. Although easy to dismiss as trivial instances of human credulity and ignorance, I suspect that such tracts are more accurately viewed as miners' canaries which we ignore at our peril. They are warning symptoms of superstition got up as religion, a refusal to extend serious thinking into the area occupied by religious questions. Such symptoms, which usually include a closed-minded and intolerant dogmatism which is happy to ride roughshod over other people's beliefs without bothering to find out what they really are, seem depressingly common. And they occur as often in the ignorant rejection of all things religious as they do in fundamentalist literature which advocates some particular point of view. Such rejections, which are of course unreasoned and unscientific, seem to have become a spiritual characteristic of our late twentieth century *Zeitgeist*. Who will not have encountered among their peers the lazy, unstudied dismissal of religion as something irrelevant to modern life? Religious illiteracy in our society has reached epidemic proportions, a matter which must clearly be of profound concern to anyone interested in religious education.

In a world where conflict situations so often have a distinctly religious dimension, with warring parties often identified simply according to their faith (Catholic and Protestant in Northern Ireland; Sikh and Hindu in the Punjab; Muslim, Jew and Christian in the Middle East), one might be forgiven for thinking that humankind would be better off without religion. But even if the value of religion *is* questioned in this way, to suggest that we could dispense with *education about religion* would seem eccentric to the point of madness. If we abandon the reasoned investigation of our religiousness, one of the most potentially explosive (and, incidentally, economically destructive) areas of human endeavour, we leave the way open for all the furies of unreason. Modern religious education tries to foster such qualities as empathy, tolerance, accurate observation and fair evaluation, and it trains the individual to think for him or herself about those great issues of life which have always moved (and which doubtless always will move) the human psyche to ponder ultimate questions about the meaning of existence, about how we ought to live in the world and behave towards each other. About what happens to us when we die. Whether those questions are pondered in a sublime or superstitious way, in a context of enlightened information or bigoted ignorance, is something which will be decided in no small part by the extent to which adequate provision is made for education in this area. Too many schools are willing to accept a level of religious education which they would not dream of imposing on any other part of the curriculum.

Christian, Buddhist, Hindu, Muslim, Humanist, Sikh, Jew or unbeliever, no matter what flag we sail the sea of life under, it is important that we all learn some elementary rules of good seamanship—which is precisely what religious education ought primarily to be about. Such rules will provide us with the necessary skills for understanding religious thought and language. Following them should give us the information needed to appreciate the cultural and historical context in which the varieties of sacred teaching have developed. They ought also to teach us a respect for other people's beliefs and provide some protection against being stranded in the shallows of fear or ignorance into which some navigation charts seem invariably to lead.

We can pity those who perished on the Herald of Free Enterprise, as we can pity the slaughtered innocents of other disasters, natural and man-made, throughout history. We can grieve with the grieving and offer any help we can, thank God or luck we were not there ourselves (or at Auschwitz or Hiroshima, Bhopal or Pompeii) and take every practical step possible to ensure that such tragedies are not repeated. But it would be wholly misplaced to try to read some sort of simplistic theological moral out of such events. All we can do in the face of such suffering is to bite on the bullet of whatever faith sustains us and realize there are no easy answers to explain away the pain that flesh is heir to, or to give us some sort of magical immunity to death. Religious education should help to ensure that, whatever bullet we bite on, it is one whose hardness has been tested by reason. Without education, we may discover that all we have to turn to when the going gets tough are shiny, empty shells which will buckle uselessly under pressure. There is a worrying dazzle and hollowness about some of the varieties of belief now flourishing among us. Worse, the bullets of faith are often used with murderous intent, rather than to sustain and guide us through life. Never has the need for proper religious education seemed more urgent.

This book attempts to paint a picture of religious education which portrays it as a necessary subject in which live issues of enormous social and personal significance are dealt with. The picture is not a finished portrait; I am neither old nor wise enough to embark on something quite so ambitious. Rather, it consists of a series of sketches which try to catch in words various perspectives on this area of educational endeavour which seems to me to be so important. Like pictures in any gallery, some will appeal more than others. I can only hope that, in at least some of my pictures, readers will find those resonances of meaning which indicate that something worthwhile has been communicated.

Modern religious education does not seek to make people religious, nor to foster scepticism. It seeks only to extend that most basic of all educational principles—the removal of ignorance—some little way into the religious realm (a realm whose history is stained with frequent explosions of barbaric intolerance and violence towards people of 'other' faiths). It involves the reasoned investigation of human religiousness in all its marvellous and fascinating diversity, rather than the unquestioning transmission of some particular faith. Its often criticized neutrality is in fact a commitment to critical openness and empathy. To look for specifically Christian (or Muslim or Hindu) teaching within it would be to mistake the very nature of the subject. Such a solecism would be rather like prospecting for gold in a mining school, insisting that mines be sunk in the classrooms where students are taught about precious metals.

The subject, religious education (or education about religion) and its subject matter, religion itself, are not the same thing and do not have the same goals (although they do, of course, have many shared concerns). That education about religion must be fair to all comers if it is to avoid misleading those exposed to it, is surely as obvious as the fact that such an approach will go against the grain of some particular religious claims to truth. No one expects a religious outlook to be expressed neutrally, but an educational study of that outlook cannot, *a priori*, accept it as true and present it as such to those who are trying to learn about it. To do so would be indoctrination rather than education. The appalling phenomenon of 'creation science' which has seeped into the school curriculum in some states in America, thanks to pressure from fundamentalist Christian groups, is surely warning enough of what can happen if we allow faith exemption from critical scrutiny.

The differences between indoctrination, education and various adjacent endeavours have been usefully clarified by John Hull:

> The instructed pupil thinks what he is told to think. The socialized pupil thinks what others think. The evangelized pupil comes to think what the evangelist thinks. The indoctrinated pupil does not think at all. The educated pupil thinks for himself.[1]

It is surely that last mentioned quality of mind—thinking for yourself—that religious education, like every other subject, must try to foster. It is a quality on which, at the end of the day, the health of any open, democratic society depends. I hope that the pages which follow may, in a modest way, encourage the reader to think independently about religious education, to bite hard and put to the test of fair and open inquiry whatever bullets of faith they use or otherwise encounter on life's journey.

Note

1   John M Hull, *Studies in Religion and Education*, Lewes: 1984, p 182.

Part I

**Eight Life-Studies:
Sketches of Religious Education
1984-1989**

These 'sketches' of religious education were drawn from life. In other words, they take as their point of departure some aspect of the subject that occurred to me in the context of the classroom (except in the case of 'The Primal Curriculum' which was written after working as a warden on a nature reserve). Except for 'Dancing Class', which appeared in the *British Journal of Religious Education*, versions of all of these sketches have appeared in the Scottish (or in the case of 'Unholy Associations' and 'Breaking the Skin Barrier', the national) edition of the *Times Educational Supplement*. In some cases I have reproduced the articles virtually unchanged, in others I have made substantial revisions. These eight life-studies do not constitute a systematic attempt at portraying the subject as a whole, but merely reflect what happened to catch my eye at the time; nor were they intended as academic studies so much as reflective, and I hope readable, narratives.

1

The Preacher Man

What, I wonder, would be the response if a religious education teacher were to present himself at the school's biology lab and suggest to the principal teacher of that subject that a visiting Lamarckian[1] spending a week with the school's Square Earth Society, should be given the opportunity of visiting a selection of biology classes, there to expound his anti-Darwinian evolutionary views.

I know the parallel is not exact, but it was one which suggested itself to me when I first learned that an evangelist was to visit the school at the invitation of a member of the biology department, and that he was to be given leave to conduct several of my S1, S2 and S3 classes during his week's stay.

Apart from the unworthy thought, which would surely have passed through all but the most saintly mind, ie '*good*, that will give me more time to prepare x, to mark y and to read z', my predominant feeling on learning of this unexpected easing of my teaching load was one of considerable vexation. Still, as things turned out, several aspects of the evangelist's visit were—at least in retrospect—highly educational.

It is an interesting indication of the change in direction witnessed in religious education over the last few decades that where once the religious education teacher could be assumed, as a matter of course, to organize assembly, run the Scripture Union, attend church regularly and generally provide an on-the-spot example of the socially accepted norms of Christian life, today, more often than not, an uneasy distance separates the religious education teacher from such aspects of the public profession of Christian faith.

The subject as a whole has shifted its emphasis from evangelism to education. Representatives of the former attitude are incredulous and outraged that those who do not go to church, who may not even believe in God, should be thought competent to teach about religion. Whilst those who represent the latter outlook are suspicious of any indoctrinatory manoeuvre by which a prescriptive teaching

3

might be smuggled into the curriculum on the unwilling back of a subject which has worked hard to shake off the last vestiges of its burden of confessionalism.

There remain, surprisingly resilient, *two* views of what religious education is all about, regardless of official statements of educational policy. One view sees it as Christian (or Muslim or Hindu) evangelizing, the other as non-partisan educating in the area of religion. Aligning myself firmly on the side of the educators, I awaited our visiting (Christian) evangelist with some apprehension.

He arrived on the Monday morning as arranged, complete with salesman's case of props. As a communicator, all but the most accomplished or complacent of teachers might have envied his skill—I most certainly did. The presentation was fascinating, fast and—technically—faultless. The artwork and conjuring tricks used to hook his audiences' attention were first rate and, once hooked, the message he put across was clear enough for anyone to follow. Even the most intractably apathetic classes seemed at least intermittently interested, responsive and amused.

The first time I saw the performance I was impressed with its speed and skill, and by the beguiling simplicity of the moral attached to each well-timed trick or story (you need God/Jesus in your life). Indeed I was sometimes momentarily lost for any convincing reason not to accept what was being offered as *THE TRUTH*. The second time I saw the performance the gaps between premise and conclusion were obvious, the third time I felt annoyance at being even momentarily duped by the slick camouflage draped over them. Thereafter I watched the pupils, not the evangelist.

Why are children so interested in what is gruesome? By far their favourite of the evangelist's tricks was the comparatively simple and uncolourful one where a small guillotine was used, first to sever a stick of chalk or a pencil and then on a volunteer's finger, though of course with harmless results. But the outcome the class imagined, acted out (and perhaps desired?) was positively bloodthirsty. The moral of this particular trick had to do with trust—ultimately in God and Jesus.

By amazing coincidence, my S1 classes had been introduced to the unlikely topic of finger amputation the week before, when I had been startled again by the evident glee with which they contemplated rather gory happenings. Their introduction to amputation was in a lesson on the beginnings of religion, when mention was made of the hand imprints found in some of the most ancient cave sanctuaries of early man.

Many archaeologists and anthropologists now think that these hand outlines, traced out on cave walls either in red (using ochre) or black (using charcoal) are evidence of sacrifices made by our distant ancestors to the shadowy spirit forces they seem to have believed in. The outlines show hands in which one, two, or even three fingers are missing—struck off as gifts to atone for some wrongdoing (whether real or imagined) or to implore the hidden powers to make things happen *thus* in some longed-for pattern (perhaps alleviation from drought or famine, or the death of an enemy, was desired).[2]

Neither my painstakingly coloured overhead projection slides of cave paintings, the filmstrip on present-day archaic beliefs (which focussed on the rituals of Australian aborigines) or investigative reconstructions of early burials, interested the classes in quite the same way as the thought of amputating a finger.

But whereas my purpose in introducing information about such sacrifice was to illustrate how potent a force religion can be in people's lives, to show how far back in history that potency extends and to explain something of the notion of sacrifice, the evangelist sought to encourage, through his trick with the model guillotine, a particular response to one interpretation of the way in which a religious dimension cuts through human life.

Why should there be any objection to aiming for such a goal in the context of the religious education class? Surely, so some might want to argue, what the evangelist had to say was more important and relevant than learning about something so remote as stone age belief.

In an ideal world, I would like to see religious education departments balancing their academic studies by calling on *representatives* of the different living faiths to visit the classroom and talk about what they believe and why they do so (and, more importantly, what practical influence their beliefs have on their lives). In that ideal world, the basic background information would have been mastered so that the classes not only had some grasp of a basic religious vocabulary, but also an understanding of the basics of symbolic language and an appreciation of the difficulties involved in expressing religious matters in words. Moreover, the representatives available would be thoughtful, enthusiastic, patient, imaginative, and used to condensing what they had to say according to the strictures imposed by the adolescence of the audience and the briefness of the time at their disposal.

All too often, in the real world, such ideal conditions are not even met halfway, so that well-meaning, but in terms of the classroom inept and incompetent, representatives of the faiths are exposed to the trivial and silly questions voiced by ignorance and prejudice. This results in Christianity, Islam, Judaism, Buddhism or whatever taking a kamikaze nose-dive through the limits of what children will accept as credible. The wreckage provides yet more groundwork for the religious education staff to clear before proceeding.

But even in an *ideal* world I would be loath to allow *evangelists* to visit the classroom. For if we assume that an evangelist's chief purpose is conversion to a particular religious point of view, whereas the role of the representative is simply to represent, to provide an example, then the latter surely has a valid classroom use which the former cannot pretend to.

Apart from my feeling of irritation at having a carefully structured programme of work interrupted—a reasonable immediate reaction, although one which often betokens a rather blinkered over-valuation of one's subject and a lamentable lack of adaptability—my more lasting and serious objections to the evangelist's trespass on my educational territory were four in number.

First, it caused confusion in the pupils' minds between his role and mine. The distinction between educating about the religious side of life and instructing in a particular religion is, given the generally low level of theological literacy in our society, a subtle one (of which parents and other teachers, let alone pupils, are often quite unaware). I still treasure the look of sheer, stunned, speechless disbelief on one headteacher's face when, in the course of an interview for a job (which, needless to say, I did not subsequently get), it became clear that I was not the committed Christian he supposed every religious education teacher must automatically be. If a (one supposes) reasonably well-educated headteacher cannot perceive the distinction between inculcating beliefs and thinking about them, then pupils are scarcely likely to, especially if evangelists are given 'air time' in what purports to be a neutral endeavour.

Having gone to considerable pains to ensure that my lessons did not contain any explicit or implicit value judgments about religion (religious education is more concerned with understanding the mechanics of such judgments than with fostering any particular set of them), the evangelist's visit was not unlike a spanner in the methodological works. Pupils turned off anything to do with religious education by the assumption that 'it's just Bible bashing' (still a depressingly common assessment of the subject), have their cherished prejudices confirmed when the evangelist walks in. You may not align yourself with what he's saying—you may even tell the classes that you can see reasons for questioning and doubting what he says—but he's in *your* classroom, teaching *your* lesson, what further evidence of complicity is needed when the suspicion of indoctrination is already so deeply ingrained in many pupils' expectations?

Second, I would like to think that I am reasonably competent in dealing with religious and philosophical ideas. After all, it is my profession to be so. Yet I was, albeit momentarily, drawn towards accepting some of the evangelist's reasoning. Its hypnotic directness and simplicity, coupled with superb presentation and insistent speed, combined to be quite disarming. But if a professional religious thinker can be disarmed, what of my almost wholly unprepared S1s and S2s? Whilst I have immense faith in the demolishing down-to-earthness of most children's resilient commonsense, I am yet concerned that a pre-packed message of considerable concentration was being forced through religious receiving equipment of only embryonic readiness. 'Spiritual rape' is a strong phrase, and one I'd rather keep for the sort of brainwashing which some of the less reputable sects are suspected of. And yet one did distinctly feel that an unfair advantage was being taken of those experienced in handling religion only in its most diluted form.

Third, I am concerned that an evangelist's visit could have exactly the opposite effect to what is, presumably, intended. Namely that it may act to turn people *away* from Christian faith. For if one of humankind's most massively impressive spiritual traditions is portrayed with the sort of gimmickry one might associate with the sale of cut-price electronic gadgets, then it (if not religion in general) risks being devalued in the eyes of those exposed to it as such. The patter of the bargain basement or the cabaret, although undoubtedly enticing and entertaining, is surely ill-suited to communicating the real value of Christianity.

Fourth, it was irritating to be left answering the questions which occurred long after the evangelist had packed his bags and gone. As the pupils began slowly to formulate objections to what had left most of them speechless at the time, I was the only one left to answer them, and was promptly cast in the role of defender of a faith I did not profess, in an intermittent cross-examination which broke into the programme of work for several weeks and tended to confuse the issues I was trying to get them to think about.

As an educator I am, of course, committed to evangelizing—for open discussion, for unswerving allegiance to the conventions of free, fair and disciplined debate, for the courage to face whatever conclusions are reached by well-informed, clear and honest thinking (even if such conclusions are at odds with the outcome we would have liked). Our evangelist seemed to infringe these principles by offering as conclusive a few special ideas which were allowed exemption from all but the most facile critical consideration. He is, of course, entitled to his views. But the religious education teacher intent on educating is surely entitled—if not, indeed, obliged—to turn down any request to use his classroom as a forum for the propagation of beliefs which seek to take root in the mind without being subjected to the normal processes of inquiry.

I would love to see closer co-operation between religious organizations and the schools. My objections to evangelism in the classroom are made with the clear realization that only the faintest idea of what being religious is all about can be conveyed in a classroom setting. The ideal might be to have some kind of religious field work to supplement and try out those strategies learned inside. I know, for example, of a Buddhist monastery in the south of England where pupils from a local school are allowed to sample week-long 'retreats' in a Buddhist setting (in Thailand such temporary monastic sojourns are a commonplace part of growing up). Topped and tailed with appropriate educational material, such periods of stay—where pupils could observe at first hand without any kind of pressure to *accept* what they see—would surely be rather more useful than what visiting evangelists can provide, or what can be learned from rushed visits to churches, mosques, synagogues and temples.

Perhaps the most profitable use which religious education can make of the evangelist of any persuasion—Christian, Hindu, Buddhist, Marxist, *etc*—is to allow such individuals to provide a testing ground for the exercising of that critical consciousness which education should, but, alas, so rarely does, inculcate in all its charges. Certainly the most fruitful aspect of our evangelist's visit, at least so far as I was concerned, came in a follow-up lesson with a very bright S3 class where we tried, with no small success, to separate the evangelist's method from his teaching and to analyse what could be said for and against presentation and what was presented. This was a useful exercise educationally, and, I think, religiously, but I fear that for most of the other classes the medium and the message formed a single, inseparable, and perhaps in the end deadly continuum, where all that glittered was as likely to be taken for gold as it was to be dismissed as mere garnish.

Notes

1   A follower of Jean Baptiste Lamarck (1744–1829). Lamarck's theories on the inheritance of acquired characteristics influenced thinking

on evolution through most of the nineteenth century and indeed survived into the twentieth century. His explanation of evolutionary change is now generally seen as erroneous, having been superseded by the Darwinian view that natural selection (not the inheritance of acquired characteristics) is the main cause of evolution.

2 For details of prehistoric finger amputation see S Giedion, *The Eternal Present, the Beginnings of Art*, London: 1962, pp 99–100.

2

The Mimicry of Faith

For the rest of the day all the classes who *hadn't* seen the ritual performed, complained loudly about the dreadful smell—demanding that windows be opened, clutching handkerchiefs over noses and feigning nausea in the time-honoured tradition of over-reaction to the slightest distraction which might postpone the work in hand.

Being surrounded by it all day, indeed for a full week, since it occurred first thing in the morning and was a repeat lesson given to all first year classes, I became so used to the smell that I ceased to notice it, thereby offering a small example of that amazing human ability to accept, or get used to, almost anything that happens—an ability which has played so importantly ambiguous a role in our history, alternating between being routinely useful, facilitating the stoically heroic and allowing the most appalling horrors to take place unchallenged.

It is only now in retrospect that the pungent, sickly-sweet aroma of incense returns to trouble my memory and to disturb my conscience with questions which *should* have been asked at the time. That they were not, I can only excuse by appeal to my status as a student teacher, considering almost all classroom experience, and in particular any new methods of approach, as providing practical grist (the more rough-hewn the better) to my fragile theoretical mill. Also, I am quite ready to confess, the ritual itself exerted a strangely captivating appeal.

Who, from among the generations who received scripture lessons of the traditional biblical type (and I count myself among them), could have guessed that religious education would become so firmly multi-faith in outlook? Could anyone raised on such staples as the journeys of St Paul have predicted that in 1984 a whole issue of the *British Journal of Religious Education* would be devoted to the teaching of *Hinduism* in this country,[1] or that replica demonstrations of Hindu rituals would be conducted by religious education teachers as a matter of course in many schools? Perhaps more than any other subject, religious education has, in the last two or three decades, gone through a metamorphosis so radical that could we summon back unchanged an experimental figure from its recent scriptural past, the chances are that they would be unable to identify large parts of their subject in its present manifestation.

Whatever factors have caused this tremendous mutation, whether it is due to the growing pluralism of society and the religious consequences radiating from the increased diversity of urban populations, or to a disillusionment with more familiar forms of religion, the change in religious education looks permanent. One striking aspect of its new identity involves the much greater demonstrative use of actual religious objects and actions.

The classroom mimicry of rituals is by no means confined to Hinduism. The necessary items for such reconstructions, whether authentic or specially made for use in schools, are now available across a range of faiths, so that the well-stocked religious education department will have its Christian, Hindu, Jewish, Buddhist and Islamic 'boxes', each filled with the appropriate artefacts. In fact, resource catalogues for religious education now often have a special section featuring such props. The first case of such mimicry which I encountered (and conducted) was, however, of a Hindu nature, so I will concentrate on it and consider some of the implications raised by a replica act of devotion to the great Indian deity Shiva, reproduced in an Edinburgh classroom with not a single Hindu among the pupils.

To anyone with any knowledge of the subject, the mind may now be preparing to boggle, because in many of his aspects Shiva is decidedly *not* the first choice one might make from the complex and colourful Hindu pantheon as an introduction to this particular area of human religiousness. Garlanded with a necklace of skulls, the cobra—deadliest of snakes—entwined about an arm, often portrayed in the accompanying mythology as raving and ithyphallic, Shiva, god of destruction, famed for extremes both of asceticism and eroticism, would surely be a rather inappropriate subject for first-year susceptibilities. Let me quickly reassure any mind about to boggle thus, that the ritual which was re-enacted in the classroom was nothing more outlandish than a simple *puja* ceremony of everyday worship such as might be performed at any Hindu family's shrine. Shiva was cast more in the role of 'Ishvara', personal Lord, than in one of his more terrible aspects.

What, exactly, did the ritual consist of? The focal point was a large colour poster of Shiva, printed in Bombay. It portrayed the god as sitting cross-legged in yogic posture, with a rather demure serpent coiled around one of his four arms. His third eye, symbolizing wisdom and power, was shown as a small enjewelled point in the middle of his forehead. Shiva's capacity to destroy was suggested by a trident, grasped in his upper right hand. Interestingly, in conformity to what is, apparently, a universal tradition in popular devotional art, even so potently fierce a deity as Shiva was depicted as a somewhat chubby and vaguely smiling youth of indeterminate sex (this last feature, incidentally, being quite accurate, for 'he' is, in fact, an androgynous god). Beneath the poster, on a table cleared of textbooks for the occasion, were a collection of cult objects: a garishly painted wooden statuette of Ganesha, Shiva's son, an elephant-headed god of good fortune; two oil lamps; incense (both joss sticks and cones, in a variety of exotic scents — sandalwood, lotus, patchouli, *etc*); yellow flower petals carefully strewn beneath the picture of Shiva; offerings of rice and spices set out in saucers; a monkey drum, to offer the praise of sound. The significance of all these items was explained, silence demanded, the incense set to smoulder, the oil lamps lit, the monkey drum sounded—and a classroom full of twelve year olds watched spellbound for some minutes at this small tableau of Hindu devotion, correct in every detail except one—*devotion*.

Now where, I hear you ask, was there any harm in such a demonstration? It's not as if anyone was actually *worshipping*, it was all done with deliberate detachment. No one was told: 'You must worship a god called Shiva like *this*', or even 'Here is an example of Hindu worship'. But merely, 'Worship in the context of Hinduism is often expressed rather like this'. All quite innocent? A good addition to the course? An effective introduction to Hindu devotion? In some ways, surely, *yes*—and yet there is a nagging sense of residual unease.

There are two areas of comparison to which useful reference can be made in order to explore this sense of unease. These may serve to explain why it arises and help to discover if it is indicative of anything much more than a vestigial superstitious loyalty to that brand of literal, fundamentalist Christianity which would condemn as idolatrous anything which moved outside of very strict guidelines (guidelines so narrow and inflexible that any train of theological thought short-sighted enough to follow them would be fated to disappear, lemming-like, over the edge of one of those intellectual precipices, the clearer perception of which in modern times has done so much to make our religious thinking more reasonable and sophisticated).

The *first* area of comparison introduces a series of positive, encouraging parallels to the demonstration ritual. Reproductions of great works of art have, for example, given increasingly widespread access to the world's aesthetic masterpieces. Are we to condemn such things as in some way undesirable? Surely no art teacher would feel unease at having reproductions of works by Rembrandt, Turner, Picasso and so on in the classroom. Should the religious education teacher feel any differently about possessing reproduction religious artefacts and using them in replica rituals designed to give increased access to, and understanding of, some of the world's *religious* masterpieces? Moreover, in drama are not all sorts of human beliefs and feelings mimicked to great educational advantage? Why should it be any different in religious education?

The *second* area of comparison introduces a series of negative, unease-increasing parallels. Replica firearms, for example, provide the enthusiast with a cheap way of collecting otherwise unobtainable weaponry—but can they not be mistaken for the real thing with quite disastrous consequences? May they not give us a false sense of security and perhaps make us careless when we come to handle a real and lethal weapon? Similarly, forged banknotes may be virtually identical to the currency they mimic, and might be used to great effect in practical exercises in basic arithmetic, but consider the wider consequence of such replication—an undermining and devaluing of the whole monetary system.

Is the use of demonstration rituals in religious education more closely akin to reproductions of famous paintings or to fakes; to drama or to forgery? Does it correspond more closely to an educative acting out or to a misleading mimicking? The argument could be turned either way, and doubtless if one felt satisfaction rather than unease in the wake of using such rituals, the *positive* parallels would be appealed to. My unease dictates a different course. I would, however, be interested to hear a statement of the opposite reaction.

For it seems to me that the net effect of performing such demonstration rituals is comparable to the introduction of forged currency, rather than to any more encouraging parallel. As such, it threatens to disturb the whole religious economy. Now this is *not* to endorse that economy and suppose that religious coins can buy goods of a sort quite unobtainable to a non-religious outlook. The religious economy *may* be considered to be bankrupt in terms of the balance of payments which it offers. Whether it is solvent or bankrupt is a matter for the philosopher, theologian and each individual believer and unbeliever to consider for themselves—it is certainly *not* something for the religious education teacher to dictate.

If we take religious objects and perform religious actions out of context, however, we surely risk a miscalculation of the worth of religion, based on an over-emphasis on its *external* dimensions. After all, what is, to the believers involved, important about ritual, cannot be brought into the classroom as easily as simply purchasing the appropriate Hindu or Islamic 'box'. Even in genuine rituals it is easy for the observer to focus attention on the symbols, rather than on what they are meant to symbolize, on the pointing finger itself, rather than that at which it is supposed to be pointing. How much easier, then, to adopt such an off-target perspective when the symbolic artefacts and actions are presented as things of *intrinsic* interest. Religious education in its modern manifestation is, I think quite rightly, neutral in terms of adopting any evaluative position concerning those purported points of transcendent reference (God, Nirvana, Brahman, the Tao, *etc*) which bring the meaning of religious rituals into focus. But such neutrality must surely not be allowed to direct the attention of the pupils to the periphery of religious experience, to the extent that they may think that this is all there is. It *may* be all there is—perhaps the transcendent points of reference are, in the end, illusory—but religious education must not act as if the question has been settled one way or the other, unless it wishes to abandon its neutral status.

Just as we might feel uncomfortable about a religious education teacher who was not a believer attending—or even organizing—school assembly (simply because this was expected of them), so too might we likewise feel that something was not quite right about conducting replica demonstration rituals in the classroom without there being any element of belief involved. For both activities introduce an element of superficiality, if not dishonesty, which surely cannot be very useful in either religious or educational terms. Regardless of the value which we personally assign to religion, we ought surely to avoid, at least in the context of the classroom, any activity whose underlying ethos has already judged the issue. The ethos of replica rituals seems seriously to infringe such a stricture.

If a volcano is thought to be extinct, few people will mind being close to it. If it is still live, their unease will be tempered by the frequency of its eruptions. Some people in our society claim that religion is extinct; all that remains, they say, is the solidified lava of misconceptions and illusions which more credulous ages took for the red-hot glow of transcendence. Others believe that it is a very live thing indeed, which can erupt into any life—often without much warning. According to who is correct, walking on the inside of the cone may be a safe or hazardous endeavour in terms of influencing one's particular outlook on the world. If religious education is to retain its neutral status then presumably it must conduct its activities from a reasonably safe distance. Do replica rituals fall into this category? Surely far from qualifying as such, they are more like exercises in excavation at the centre of the crater.

In a religious context, rituals are used precisely as formalized reminders of those points of contact with some transcendent entity or state which gives religion the sense it claims. In imitating such rituals we are surely assuming either that no such points of contact exist, or that we don't mind exposing pupils to them, or that ritual forms have no great mnemonic efficacy. None of these assumptions seem consonant with the neutral standpoint of present-day religious education. Moreover, simply by taking such rituals out of context and performing them in an everyday classroom setting, we are almost bound to render mundane what is, in its proper context, sacred and set apart.

Without harking back to some sort of silly theological literalism which would see a Hindu deity such as Shiva as existing in giant humanoid form with four arms and the rest of the iconographic gear, a figure who, if called upon even in the most superficial replica ritual might appear genie-like in a puff of smoke and make us all devotees, there is still, I think, a very real sense in which replicating rituals may be playing with fire. Of course a key aim of any religious education teacher must surely be to burn away that dreadful apathy which prejudges this whole subject area, in such an offhand and arrogantly ignorant way, as something boring and useless. Perhaps the ignition of a blaze of interest and excitement via some colourful practical dimension is just what is needed. The trouble is, it's easier to start a fire than to stop it spreading in directions in which we might not want it to go (after all, if we allow the replication of one ritual, just where do we draw the line?). Certainly, from my own experience of one seemingly innocuous replicated ritual, I can see a veritable cloud of smoke emerging in which the still uncertain philosophy of the subject could easily become lost and we might well find ourselves leading those in our charge down a hazardous path in a highly dubious direction.

Note

1   The *British Journal of Religious Education*, vol 6 no 3 (Summer 1984), special issue on 'Teaching Hinduism Today'.

3

Unholy Associations

Immediate associations and chance remarks are often instructive in a way that eludes our more deliberate utterances. They give away what we *really* think about something underneath the reserve which more studied reflection tends to impose.

Some subjects are particularly apt to break through to that primeval part of our personality whose voice shouts out in these un-thought instant responses. Politics and religion are, traditionally, the most direct routes to this subterranean alter ego and, as such, are taboo subjects at those dinner tables where reason's veneer is preferred to the depths of gut-reaction.

Anyone who is professionally concerned with religion, unless they move in the most refined circles, will have experienced scores of instantly expressed opinions about their chosen subject, opinions which are often comical, sometimes sad and occasionally terrifying in the wider implications of the ignorance they betray. Whatever shape such sudden baring of true feeling takes, however, it is highly instructive and can be deliberately elicited in the class-room as a rough indicator of how much prior knowledge religious education can assume, or how much education it has achieved.

One of the more memorable off-the-cuff remarks about religion which I have encountered was made by a plain-clothes security man on the ferry between Stranraer and Larne. It was during the height of 'the troubles' in the early 1970s, when all non-tie-wearing slightly scruffy young males travelling to Northern Ireland were liable to be questioned at some length. When he learned that I was a student he asked what subject I was studying. On hearing 'Religious Studies' he immediately looked at the magazine lying open on the table in front of me (Punch) and said with a wink, 'Then I don't think you should be reading *that*'. What, one won-ders, would have met with his approval? Calvin's *Institutes*, the *Bhagavad Gita*? What would he have thought of that most reli-gious of modern comedies, *The Hitch-Hiker's Guide to the Galaxy*? One fears that only an open Bible, a grimly unsmiling face and the general demeanour of an undertaker would have satisfied his expectations. When the topic of religion came up, his first reaction to it revealed a compound confusion between studying religion and being religious, and between being religious and having no sense of humour.

A more common response to the revelation that one is somehow involved with religion, whether as teacher or student, takes roughly the following form. *Question*; 'What do you do?'; *answer*: 'I'm a religious education teacher' (or 'student of religious studies'); *response*: (with varying degrees of rage) 'Well, what I want to know is this, if there's a God why did he make the world like this? Why is it such a cruel, unjust place? Go on, tell me, why does he allow such suffering to happen?' Since this is something which has always puzzled me, and seems to stand as an immovable obstacle in the path of any simple, paternalistic image of deity (it may, in fact, entirely block the logical road to some concepts of deity), I am unable to provide any satisfactory reply. Indeed, on encountering such a scenario, I tend to express agreement and even to amplify the problem, presenting—via Augustine's well-honed formulation— the cutting edge with which it threatens the jugular of Christian theism ('Either God cannot prevent evil or he will not; if he cannot, he is not all-powerful; if he will not, he is not all-good'). Such a response does not generally meet with the approval of those whose first reaction is to cast me in the role of defender of a faith they have rejected. I become instead some sort of turncoat, a traitor who betrays the defence they seem to desire. For, intriguingly, many of those who react to religion/religious education in this way appear not to like too much to be said against the God they don't believe in. One is reminded of Yossarian's bizarre theological encounter with Lieutenant Scheisskopf's wife in Joseph Heller's marvellous novel *Catch 22*. After his inimitable expression of the problem of belief, given the existence of suffering in the world, she, although an avowed atheist, bursts into tears. When the perplexed Yossarian asks her why she is so upset, she replies, 'the God I don't believe in is a good God, a just God, a merciful God. He's not the mean and stupid God you make him out to be'.[1] Like many who apparently reject religion, Lieutenant Scheisskopf's wife tries to smuggle in a half-belief under the guard of insufficiently examined difficulties. Her discomfort becomes intense when those difficulties are more closely examined.

Those who imagine that religious education must be ready, able and willing to justify the ways of God to man, betray once more a failure to distinguish between being religious and studying religion. This unfortunate confusion is complicated by the assumption that religion automatically implies God and that believers can either neatly explain away suffering, or else simply fail to notice its occurrence—the implication then being that they must be credulous or blind. It comes as an uncomfortable shock to such simplistic outlooks to discover that religion can be atheistic and that within its theistic strands there is a long theological tradition which deals with the problem of evil in an intellectually rigorous fashion.

Classroom gut-reactions are, of course, legion and one could fill many pages recording them. One of the more unexpected which I recall was from an S2 girl who, midway through a resource-based unit on Islam, piped up with, 'When are we going to do some *proper* religious education, sir?' Her expectations would probably have been satisfied by much the same blueprint as the security man at Stranraer appeared to have in mind. What she said is evidence of a widespread identification of religion with Christianity (and usually with one fairly narrow understanding of it at that). This common solecism, which reads 'Christianity' for 'religion', rules out of court as irrelevant, if not mistaken—and at any event beyond the pale of *proper* religious education—the faith of Hindus, Buddhists, Muslims and all the other non-Christian believers in the world. Such an outlook seems singularly inappropriate, not to say dangerous, on our increasingly inter-conscious religiously plural planet.

Although it would not do to read too much into them, chance remarks tend to suggest that, at a very fundamental level, ignorance about religion is commonplace. In terms of the population as a whole, it sometimes seems as if we are perilously close to becoming a religiously illiterate nation. One of the difficulties in remedying the situation lies in the continuing problem of assessing competence in this area. After all, it is relatively easy to determine the degree of someone's competence in English (or Greek, or chemistry or physics), but how exactly do we measure literacy when it comes to religion? The introduction of certificate exams has helped to some extent. Yet a feeling of unease persists—have we really got much beyond measuring mere factual informedness? Similarly, whilst the *consequences* of linguistic or scientific illiteracy are obvious—people are unable to follow simple instructions, things stop working—the consequences of religious illiteracy are not easy to see until they get altogether out of hand. Perhaps if they were more obvious at an earlier stage, the violence in so many of the world's trouble spots would not have such a marked 'religious' basis.

Given the huge reservoir of ignorance about religion which is suggested by the spot-checks provided through the medium of chance remarks, religious education teachers are faced with an immense remedial task. Before they can move on with any

confidence to more advanced levels, they must first try to deal
with gut-level reactions which make those in their charge unwilling
or unable to see beyond the horizons of their own prejudice. The
resources needed to effect such a sea-change are immense. As one
Deputy Head put it to me in a highly revealing aside, 'Ideally, I
think a religious education teacher should be an ex-boxer with the
patience of a saint'. Since his school's religious education 'department' was housed on two shelves in the cupboard of an outlying
corridor, since no room was set aside for the religious education
class, since there was no syllabus and no specialist staff, I was
inclined to agree with him. Anyone taking up the post he was
interviewing for would need to repair to the gym quite frequently
to work out their frustrations on a punchball. Alternatively, they
might need a saint's patience to endure the life-sentence which
would doubtless have been meted out after they had finished with
those who refused to take the relatively simple, practical steps
which could have done so much to remedy the situation. Alas, I
did not feel that I measured up to the job description, either in
physique or temperament, and would suspect that the aforesaid
Deputy and his team are still watching the skies over Edinburgh
wondering if the superman they seem to require will have hung up
his gloves and sensed his true vocation. Barry McGuigan where are
you?

If anyone doubts the accuracy of this rather pessimistic view of
people's religious education, as indicated by their chance remarks
about matters connected with religion (what on earth, one wonders, were they *taught*?), let them experiment with deliberately
elicited instant responses in the classroom. If pupils are asked
to write down (or, more courageously, to speak out) an instant
response to the word 'religion' or to 'religious education', an
enormous venting of gut-feeling and confusion tends to occur in
the associations they arrive at. Dismissing those merely antagonis-
tic replies calculated to annoy and looking at genuine outbursts
only, the picture is unlikely to be encouraging. In my experience
(limited and hopefully unrepresentative) the ensuing associations
show chronic confusion between religion and religious education.
The latter is simply seen as a vehicle (driven by an interested
party) for bulldozing those in its path towards the former. Religious education is thus resisted as attempted indoctrination. Even
more depressing, 'religion' tends to elicit 'God' and 'boring' in
about equal measure, with little variation on so unimaginative a
theme (the basis, perhaps, for a theology of accidie?). Taking the
association game a stage further towards deliberation, it is often
interesting to ask a class to spend five or six minutes answering

two simple questions. One asks for a definition of religion, the other for an evaluation of its right to a place on the school curriculum. A common outcome is an inability to define religion beyond the most garbled confusion of higgledy-piggledy pseudo-Christian ideas. Unsurprisingly, if this is what they take it to be, religion is thought to be undeserving of any place on the school timetable.

The Religious Experience Research Unit at the University of Nottingham (whose mother unit at Oxford was the brain-child of the zoologist Sir Alister Hardy) was responsible for a project to research and develop a curriculum programme of experiential learning in religious education at both primary and secondary levels. At a course for teachers who had been participating in the work, the attitudes of those present to 'religion' and 'spirituality' were investigated by what was rather alarmingly referred to as 'brainstorming'. In fact this is less dramatic than it sounds and simply involves looking at the immediate responses which certain words conjure up in the mind. Among the responses called out to 'religion' were: processions, rules, old men, fanatics, our old friend boredom (surprise, surprise . . .) and, intriguingly, old ladies in frilly hats. Among the responses to 'spirituality' were: depth, mystery, peace, bliss, darkness, holiness and energy. The result of such deliberate brainstorming tends to confirm what a more random exploration of immediate responses would suggest; 'religion' has some rather unholy associations in many people's minds.[2]

Aldous Huxley once remarked that it was a great pity we couldn't dry-clean words.[3] 'Love' was one he particularly singled out as dirty linen waiting for the laundress. Its mis- and over-use had, in Huxley's eyes, left it tangled up with all the wrong sorts of connotations and unable to speak its intended meaning. Before it could perform its proper function a period of cleansing and disinfection was required. If we could only apply some such process to 'religion' and 'religious education', we might dodge those gut-feelings, those instant and ignorant associations, which the very words seem to trigger in so many minds, and begin the vital process of religious education unhindered by the immense dead-weight which unchallenged prejudice imposes on any attempted advancement of learning in this area.

Perhaps the experiential approach pioneered by the Religious Experience Research Unit will one day issue in some profound change of attitude—so that eventually every unhelpful negative association will be eliminated. Since the work there is explicitly geared to going beyond the public phenomena of religion (which seem to elicit such bad feeling) and getting to the inner experiential root out of which the religious impulse in *Homo sapiens* apparently arises, one hopes that it might be successful. Fears that such roots may have been buried beyond reach in the accumulated boredom with, and rejection of, religion evident in so many who attend religious education classes, ought to be calmed by the Unit's findings concerning the common incidence of some form of spiritual experience in modern British society.[4] Moreover, any worries that an experiential approach might lead back to some sort of confessionalism should be allayed by a declared intention to eschew evangelism of any sort and stick to the straight and narrow of an educational approach. Promising though it may be, however, it will doubtless be some time before such useful work bears any very tangible fruit.

In the meantime, 'brainstorming' and the instant reactions it elicits, plus the similar insights offered by casual chance remarks, can provide useful dipsticks to test the nature of deep-seated feelings about religion. I do not imagine that the readings they show will change much in my lifetime; all the indications from the bore-holes I've chanced upon or dug suggest that massive surgery, rather than linguistic dry-cleaning, is what is required. But of course that requires massive resources, and one suspects that when religious education is voiced in the corridors of power, whether educational or political, the responses are 'non-priority', 'unimportant' or, as one member of an influential committee is rumoured to have said, 'why can't it just go away?' The work done by the Religious Experience Research Unit is a small light in an area of considerable darkness. Until further illumination dawns (ushered in, perhaps, by that superhumanly patient ex-boxer?) we will doubtless continue to be treated to the spectacle of apparently well-educated people reverting to some atavistic level of ignorance and barbarism as soon as the word 'religion' is mentioned. It is a metamorphosis whose Jekyll and Hyde potential overshadows its more light-hearted occurrences.

Notes

1   Joseph Heller, *Catch 22*, London: 1962, p 195.
2   The results of this 'brainstorming' on 'religion' and 'spirituality' are contained in *Inside Information*, published by the Religious Experience Research Unit, April 1985.
3   Aldous Huxley, *Eyeless in Gaza*, Harmondsworth: 1974, p 14.
4   See David Hay, *Exploring Inner Space*, Harmondsworth: 1984.

4

A Christmas Story

Story-telling must surely rank as one of the more respectable contenders for the title 'oldest profession'—and it is certainly an art of which it may truly be claimed that 'age cannot wither her, nor custom stale her infinite variety'. Alas, for some people, age seems to constitute something of an impasse to their enjoyment and instruction via this particular medium, for there is a deeply entrenched belief that stories are for children and that when we grow up we grow beyond them. What might be called the 'once upon a time syndrome' tars all stories with the brush of the nursery. Yet even if we stick to such a simple form as the fable, leaving to one side the tales of Jesus, Socrates, Buddha and other great story-tellers, it is surely clear that what we are dealing with is far from child's play. It would be a bizarre misapprehension to suppose that Aesop and La Fontaine were concerned to address their wisdom exclusively to the under tens. Quite apart from anything else, we should remember that La Fontaine drew most of the subjects of his second volume of fables from an ancient Indian bestiary, the Pancatantra, which belongs to a tradition of political philosophy ruthless enough to make Machiavelli seem almost innocent—hardly the stuff that nursery tales are made of.

Christmas is, of course, the story-telling season par excellence. Almost inevitably, in a few days of annual sentimentality, the normal staple diet of TV viewing is displaced and interrupted by such favourites as Dickens' *Christmas Carol* and Wilde's *The Selfish Giant*, whilst Christmas card illustrators make scores of cameo scenes suggestive of all sorts of cosy winter tales—sleigh bells, robins, snowmen, log fires and holly berries. And of course somewhere, underneath all the decorations, turkey and present-buying, there is *the* Christmas story. Thus, as the tinsel and fairy lights encroach ever earlier into December, and we are given countdowns on the number of shopping days left as if our very existence depended on it, religious education teachers are likely to find themselves prevailed upon by pupils to 'tell us a story', and/or to find that their own thoughts are turning independently in this direction—especially as it becomes clear just how remote from the occasion which it supposedly celebrates the whole seasonal jamboree has become. So, as the Christmas term draws to a close, variants on 'Once upon a time in Bethlehem' are likely to be heard in classrooms up and down the country.

Why should the prospect of such harmless story-telling fill me with the deep unease it does? Surely teaching, and religious education teaching above all, must try to address topical issues, try to capture interest by dealing with things which have some present, tangible effect on pupils' lives. And in December, whose consciousness can remain unassailed by some aspects of the Christmas spectacular which lays siege to our senses? Surely it is quite apt to remind ourselves of where it all started, of what the celebrations were actually intended to mark before the retailers latched on to them and rampant consumerism took over.

There is no denying the usefulness of the ancient art of story-telling in religious education. Stories can often get a point across with an economy which simply leaves bankrupt more laborious non-narrative approaches. Good stories exhibit more readily than many learned works something of what Whitehead, in *The Aims of Education*, saw as the last acquirement of the educated mind, namely a sense for style—the feeling for the direct attainment of ends simply, directly and without waste.[1] In the parables of Jesus, creation stories from primitive religions, Hindu and Buddhist tales—indeed across the whole spectrum of religion—obscurities of doctrine, tangles of history and philosophy, impenetrabilities of language and location, suddenly give way to the simple, lucid light of stories. Their use tends to be uncomplicated and effective, the interest they create is strong, and the instruction they provide well nigh spontaneous (if also ephemeral). The effectiveness of story in conveying something of the negative side of the numinous, such things as ghosts and hauntings, has long been recognized. But the more positive aspects of human religiousness are also readily accessible by this means of approach. Moreover, as the subject has expanded over recent decades to take in 'world religions', the religious education teacher has access to a growing treasure-trove of stories. Why should anyone feel a sense of disquiet at the thought of using such excellent educational devices?

If more assurance of their worth is necessary beyond the criterion of being tried and tested in the classroom and found *to work* there (a rare enough accolade), there are many indications that story-telling as a method has been granted 'official' recognition of worth by those whose job it is to consider the more theoretical aspects of religious education. Thus the Summer 1982 issue of the

British Journal of Religious Education, always a good indicator of the profession's thoughts, was entirely devoted to religious education through story.[2] In fact the issue was virtually a festschrift to honour story as one of the oldest and most useful arts of the religious educator. Likewise, the Shap Working Party on World Religions in Education, in its excellent 1977 *Handbook for Teachers*, commends the use of story and contains an interesting section on the use of the novel in religious education.[3]

There are, I think, two main reasons why I feel uneasy about the use of stories in religious education, despite their proven classroom effectiveness and the theoretical blessing which their use has received. The unease makes me quite resistant to all blandishments to tell a story, unless the ground has been properly prepared beforehand.

First, there is a seeming inability on the part of many members of our society to recognize that a story may still be valuable even if it isn't *true*. The creation story in Genesis is, perhaps, the classic example here. In a scientized, technicized world such as this, it is a foolhardy teacher who confronts a class head-on with what they will see as a series of evident absurdities. 'In seven days, sir? That's just silly.' Moreover, attempts to establish the value of such a story after the event of its apparent factual disgrace, are apt to look all too like desperate face-saving attempts. Unless something of the nature and value of mythological thinking has been made clear to a class *before* they are confronted with an example of it, it is almost inevitable, given the assumptions which are inbred in our society, that the story in question will be subjected to instant ridicule and disbelief, which totally obscures the point that factual accuracy is not the only criterion by which to assess the truth and significance which a story may carry.

Our cultural ineptitude when it comes to understanding mythological material, is well illustrated by the delightful incident recorded by Mary Douglas in *Purity and Danger*, her famous study of concepts of pollution in primitive societies.[4] Once, when a band of Bushmen had performed their rain rituals, a small cloud appeared on the horizon. It grew and darkened and soon rain fell. But the anthropologists who were present as observers, and who asked if the Bushmen reckoned that the rite had actually produced the rain, were simply laughed out of court by the tribesmen, who were amazed at the simplistic absurdity into which their one-track cause and effect thinking had led them. How naïve can we get, Douglas asks along with the Bushmen, about the beliefs of others? In much the same way, many children seem to think that the only purpose a story has is to relate what happened (an odd idea when one considers what they watch on TV). If a story is self-evidently fantastic, improbable, or disproved by some nugget of scientific information—which they often clutch tightly and superstitiously to as a talisman—then it is simply dismissed as 'silly' and perceived as having no value, or as being of only nursery-room relevance and thus beneath mature dignity to consider as having something important or interesting to say. Until some clear sense of their non-documentary value has been recognized, it can be highly counter-productive to expose pupils to stories which are easily ridiculed or 'disproved' by reference to crude positivistic criteria.

Second, and far more difficult to remedy, before many religious stories can begin to make any sort of sense, one has to try to ensure that people can see what they are getting at (which is, of course, *quite* different from getting them to believe in them). Just as there is not much point explaining fire-drill to someone who has no concept of the dangers posed by fire, so it can be similarly pointless introducing people to religious teachings if they have absolutely no idea what the sense of danger is against which they are being offered as antidote.

If the world is seen as being a wholly self-sufficient and explicable phenomenon, as somewhere secure, predictable and unmysterious, many religious stories will never have a chance to get off the ground. In a world of presents, turkey and tinsel, where the religious dimension of life tends often to be obscured by an intrusive materialism which proclaims 'all's well' via the irresistible stridency of well-advertised consumer durables, questions relating to the purpose of life, to human destiny, to individual and ultimate responsibilities, life after death and suffering, are likely to fall on deaf ears. How could such deafness hear any significance in the story of the birth of a redeeming world saviour? In such a world, the concept of salvation has no place. As Thomas Merton mused in the preface to a book of meditative essays, some people today have simply stopped asking themselves the traditional questions which lie at the root of most religious thinking.[5] The virgin birth, the three wise men, the shepherds and the star seem to stick in the throat of an untutored modern mind. They are too much for it to interpret beyond an instant dismissal as fantastic. Without careful preparatory work, Oh little town of Bethlehem has little hope of survival in the urban enormities of the twentieth century.

Unless you see life as something which is in some way problematic, peculiar, mysterious, precariously transient and replete with questions, the existence of answers to questions thus automatically posed will not be a matter of particular interest. Our present culture often seems simply to have drowned out the timeless interplay of such question and answer in our religious consciousness with the sheer din of productivity and consumerism. The Christmas story, indeed almost every religious story I can think of, is reliant to some extent on the supposition that, even if people do not agree with the cure which is offered, they recognize that any serious assessment of the human condition must result in the verdict of a serious ailment requiring attention.

Religious stories might be seen as being addressed to situations where we are aware of skating on perilously thin ice over unfathomable depths of unanswered, troubling questions about who we are, what we ought to be doing and where we are going. Our twentieth century technocracy seems to have frozen our spiritual sensibilities rock solid, so that we often forget what lies beneath our feet and where our steps are leading us. The thin ice of the surface seems metres thick, many do not even seem to realize that there is not endless solidity beneath us. Day to day comfort and luxuries have blinded us to the limitations of mere material well-being.

So, perhaps rather than getting preoccupied with snowflakes, Santa Claus and all the other hackneyed reinforcements to the permafrost of our materialism, we should, come December, turn our thoughts instead to the warmer climes of India and let Eastern wisdom thaw out our frozen spirituality so that we can regain a sensitivity to some of the questions and answers which still, despite our neglect of them, must deeply concern us. In the light of these reflections, let me commend the following tale as a story suitable for laying the groundwork before the Christmas story (or virtually any other religious story, for that matter) is presented to a class. The story is too old to have retained the name of its original teller, but one famous version of it occurs in the work of Haribhadra, a seventh century Indian writer.[6] If it has a familiarity one would not expect from an ancient tale retold in the writings of one of India's lesser-known heterodox religions (Haribhadra was a Jain), it is probably because Tolstoy was so deeply impressed by it that he cited it at length in his *Confessions*. Thus any qualms about introducing an Eastern fable of doubtful provenance which are not stilled by the qualities of the story itself, might be lulled by remembering Walter Kaufmann's remark that Tolstoy is more important for the history of religion in the twentieth century than any theologian.[7] A point on which I'm sure many theologians would whole-heartedly agree.

In very condensed form, the story goes thus: A certain man was wandering through the countryside far from home. Suddenly he comes on a wild elephant which, seeing him, gives chase, trumpeting ferociously. Desperate to escape, the man looks round frantically for some place of sanctuary. There is a massive tree growing close by, so he makes for it. As he gets nearer to it, however, he realizes with dismay that its branches are too far off the ground for him to grab hold of, and so swing himself up to safety. But at the foot of the tree there is an old well. Terrified by the closeness of the elephant, the man jumps into this apparent haven. As he falls, he reaches out his hand and grabs hold of some vegetation growing from the wall of the well about half-way down. For a moment he thinks he is safe. But when he begins to take his bearings he sees that below, at the bottom of the well, there is a giant serpent waiting to consume him when he falls. Not only are his arms tiring, but the plant from whose fronds he is hanging precariously is being gnawed at by two mice, one white, one black. It is only a matter of time until he falls. Meanwhile, back on ground level, the elephant continues to charge madly about. In its rage it knocks against the tree which is growing above, and whose upper branches overhang, the well. A bees' nest is knocked down and it falls on the man's head. He is stung by a swarm of angry bees. But a drop of honey trickles into his mouth and, in the moment of tasting its flavour, he forgets all the dangers which surround him and is lost in the enjoyment of its sweetness . . . .

I have used the story—given here in barest outline—with many classes, over a wide range of age and ability. By and large, the moral (or *a* moral, for it is dense with possible meanings) dawns with some force on all but the most resolutely inattentive. It has also provided the basis for some truly marvellous illustrations which I would love to see reproduced as pre-Christmas Christmas cards. As a classroom exercise in the interpretation of symbolism, and as an example of how a story can be valuable even if it is not true, the story of the man in the well is, to my mind, superb. The picture of life it offers is not a happy one—but then if life was a wholly happy business we could dispense with Hinduism, Buddhism, Judaism, Christianity, Islam and all the other sacred teachings of the world. After all, as has often been pointed out, there would be no need for religion in paradise. In one possible reading of the story, the elephant is death, the tree stands for salvation, the well itself as a metaphor for human life, the two mice are day and night, whose serial gnawing is the saw of time working its way across the stem of the plant which represents an individual's lifespan. In such a precarious situation, what are we to do? Just concentrate on savouring the honey and try to forget where we are? Cower in fear and wait for the inevitable to happen? Or try to make our way, slowly and with difficulty, towards a more secure situation?

Of course it is rather a hazardous endeavour to use the heat of Indian wisdom to melt through the ice of our Western snow-blindness about religious issues. It is an exercise somewhat akin to sawing off a branch whilst we're still sitting on it. For modern-day religious education is not in the business of providing answers and instant comfort. When we fall into deep waters it will not instantly throw a lifebelt and come to our rescue. Rather, it will point to a variety of possible lifelines and offer advice about how to assess which might be reliable. But at the end of the day, choice is left to each individual (and it could be a matter of some importance that the *right* choice is made—remember that giant serpent! remember the gnawing teeth of time!).

One of the strongest and most durable lifelines, one that has proved itself buoyant even in the most sinking and hopeless situations (such as, precisely, that of the man in the well), was thrown to us some two thousand years ago in Bethlehem in the kingdom of Judea. For many in our classrooms, and in society at large, it has sunk to the very bottom of a frozen ocean, across whose icy surfaces we wheel our shopping trolleys, stacked with all the distracting honey which a wealthy society can offer. It is perhaps symbolic of the new age of inter-religious consciousness which has dawned, that Eastern wisdom may help to thaw a passage towards it. Whether or not, when we reach it, it will bear us to safety is, however, quite a different story.

Notes

1   Alfred North Whitehead, *The Aims of Education and Other Essays*, London: 1932, p 19f.
2   *British Journal of Religious Education*, vol 4 no 3 (Summer 1982), special issue on 'Religious Education through Story'. Some further thoughts on the usefulness of stories in religious education can be found on pp 118-122.
3   W Owen Cole (ed), *World Religions, a Handbook for Teachers*, prepared by the Shap Working Party on World Religions in Education, London: 1977, pp 42-56.
4   Mary Douglas, *Purity and Danger*, London: 1966, p 58.
5   Thomas Merton, *Raids on the Unspeakable*, London: 1977, p 2.
6   An English translation of the relevant section of Haribhadra's Story of Samaraditya (*Samaradityakatha*, 2.55-2.80) is given in Wm Theodore de Bary (ed), *The Sources of Indian Tradition*, vol 1, New York: 1958, pp 53-5.
7   Walter Kaufmann (ed), *Religion from Tolstoy to Camus*, New York: 1964, p 1.

5

Breaking the Skin Barrier

It is an instructive exercise for the religious education specialist to ask S1 classes at the beginning of their first term to identify an assortment of symbols, both sacred and secular. The results are often such as to cheer the heart of the advertiser and shatter the complacency of those who might suppose that religious values are somehow automatically transmitted from generation to generation.

If my experience is anything to go by, it seems that we are living in a society in whose schools the symbols of organizations like, say, the United Nations, or the Commission for Racial Equality, are virtually unknown compared to the various logos and liveries of a host of consumer products. Coca Cola's 'dynamic contour curve', for example, seems to be a universally recognized emblem. What sort of value-environment are our children growing up in when their awareness is geared according to such priorities? (And of course this 'Coca Cola syndrome' extends far beyond S1.)

Although the cross of Christianity may pose no problem of identification, the burning bush will almost certainly cause consternation, whilst the wheel of Buddhism, crescent of Islam, star of David and swords of Sikhism tend to produce inspired (but erroneous) guesswork—although clearly this response will vary around the country. Is it more important that we should know some rudimentary facts about the faiths which surround us, or that we are able to recite the names of a dozen brands of chocolate bar?

Consumer advertising seems to reach those parts of our retention that more serious matters rarely manage to touch. Disturbingly few S1 pupils can list the basic teachings of *any* religion, but almost without exception they know that beanz meanz Heinz, that a Mars a day helps you work, rest and play, and so on. What sort of citizens are in the making when a mish-mash of fatuous advertising jingles comes more readily to mind than any more serious code of values?

The Ten Commandments, the Sermon on the Mount, the Noble Eightfold Path, the Five Pillars—the various fundamental formulas of faith which seek to guide human life—seem in our society to be eclipsed by catch-phrases from an advertising catechism which is drilled into our consciousness by insistent media repetition. Such a situation surely has some worrying social, educational and religious implications.

Of course I am *not* suggesting that religious education should be concerned with *inculcating* religious values and that its classroom evangelism ought therefore to be pursued more aggressively to counter the challenge from the values propagated by advertising. Religious education is about education, *not* evangelism. But it is education towards understanding the values which the world's religious traditions attach to life. Unless it is to accept a situation where the subject matter it deals with is rendered conceptually invisible to its pupils, religious education must, I think, give some attention to the values which advertising extols and which threaten to shout down by sheer volume, rather than by cogent argument, any alternative way of looking at things.

In his *Four Arguments for the Elimination of Television*, Jerry Mander described advertising as a system designed 'to break the skin barrier'.[1] Once inside, advertising seeks to 're-shape feelings and create more appropriate ones'—appropriate, that is, in terms of making us buy some product. Often enough it seems that the system is effective and a host of images and nugatory imperatives lodge persistently beneath our skin.

To some extent, of course, education shares with advertising the desire to capture an audience's attention and lodge images, ideas, values deep in the psyche. There is, however, an important difference. For whilst education operates for the common good and addresses its audience through reason, appealing to the pupils' intelligence, advertising cuts this awkward corner and, operating only for commercial gain, addresses our considerable impressionability. Abandoning all but the most nominal lip-service to rationality, it aims for the eyes rather than the intellect and bombards us with a veritable armada of value-laden imagery.[2] Thus (to quote from one of their recent 'personal' letters) the American Express Card is not just a small greenish square of embossed plastic which facilitates credit, but something by which you 'tell the world—and yourself—you've made it'. Such pompous, egocentric (and, when you stop to think about it, quite ridiculous) values are attached to a whole variety of products from cigarettes to cars, from drinks to toilet paper, via a kind of technicolour mythology. In buying them we display our elegance, superiority, good taste and so on.

I am not denying for a moment that consumer ads are often amusing, usually very well made and occasionally informative. As such, there are grounds for seeing them in a more positive light in terms of the entertainment, aesthetic and information value which they offer. Moreover, there are surely abundant guidelines to regulate their use and prevent any *intolerably* illegitimate sales technique from being foisted on an unsuspecting public. But is this enough to allow the predominance they have achieved in modern society?

The British Code of Advertising Practice states as one of its general rules that:

No advertisement, whether by inaccuracy, ambiguity, exaggeration, omission or otherwise, should mislead consumers about any matter likely to influence their attitude to the advertised product.[3]

But from the point of view of most religious codes of value, surely *all* advertisements fall foul of this requirement. From almost any religious perspective I can think of, the problems which advertising presents as in need of a solution (getting rid of dandruff, achieving an even whiter wash, finding ever softer toilet paper, and so on) are simply irrelevant and serve only to distract us from the more important business of 'right living'. Moreover, in showing problem situations which are invariably solved by acquiring some product, advertisements serve also to obscure the existence of those apparently insoluble existential problems (time, suffering, death, meaning, *etc*) which are the concern of religion.

Are the advertising safeguards enough to ensure that a totally erroneous picture does not emerge on our TV screens and in the pages of our papers and magazines? Is the worldview which is presented in the scores of sentimental scenarios on TV, where beautiful, young, successful people (by far the dominant group in advertising's world) solve pseudo-problems by recourse to purchase, adequately countered by the education which our children receive? Since religious education is centrally concerned with the study of value-systems, there is surely a case to be made for it giving some attention to the picture of the world purveyed by advertising. In fact, if religious and moral values are not considered side by side with (and as a challenge to) advertising's values, it seems only a matter of time before we produce a generation that will be blind to all but a consumer's vision of the world.

Marshall McLuhan believed that one day 'education will become recognized as civil defence against media fallout'.[4] Part of the task of religious education ought surely to consist of alerting those in its charge to the fallout from advertising's vision of the world which, if we become contaminated, threatens grotesquely to distort our perception of values and distract our attention from the urgent realities—religious, political, economic, social—of the human situation

In the thirty second dreams which are the currency of TV advertising, no mention is ever made of the animals killed to ensure the safety of some new cosmetic; the pollution which is a side effect of producing a particular kind of container; the appalling foreign employment practices (offending against any religious or ethical outlook) of some of the multinationals who supply us with tea and coffee; the people who will starve because of the agricultural policy which allows us to afford and enjoy certain foods; or the colossal sums which, in a world of *real* human need, are squandered in facilitating the continuance of this weird dreamtime. (Global spending on advertising is reckoned to stand at some 200 *billion* dollars a year—more than 500 million a day.[5]) Do such omissions not mislead consumers about the products advertised, about the lives they lead, about the world they live in?

The trouble is that a critique of advertising soon brings us into conflict with some of the founding assumptions of our culture about production and wealth. Moreover, the rhetoric of compulsory entertainment, and the triviality it brings in its wake, will soon raise its head if we suggest that public channels of mass communication could, perhaps, be used in a more socially constructive way than at present. Clearly religious education cannot hope to take on such imponderables. It can, however, begin to foster a critical awareness of the advertising values which are all around us and encourage pupils to compare them with religious and moral values, and to think hard about which offer a better picture of the world. It is time we made an eye-catching educational drama out of what has all the dimensions of a spiritual crisis, instead of passively allowing our skin barrier to be broken by a value-system that reason and compassion would surely combine in rejecting.

Notes

1   Jerry Mander, *Four Arguments for the Elimination of Television*, Brighton: 1980, p 124.

2   As Neil Postman has observed, 'the distance between rationality and advertising is now so wide that it is difficult to remember that there once existed a connection between them'. (*Amusing Ourselves to Death, Public Discourse in the Age of Show Business*, London: 1987, p 131).

3 *British Code of Advertising Practice*, London: 1985 (seventh edition), paragraph 5.1.

4 Marshall McLuhan, *Understanding Media*, London: 1987 (Ark paperback edition), p 305. *Understanding Media* was first published in 1964.

5 These figures are taken from '"Develop a desire": on the ethics of global advertising', editorial article in *Media Development*, vol 34 no 3 (1987), p 1.

6

The Primal Curriculum

In E M Forster's *A Room with a View*, there is a marvellous scene when, walking together in the countryside, Lucy Honeychurch admits to Cecil, her unsuccessful suitor, that when she pictures him it is always indoors, in a drawing room with no view.[1] The unfortunate Cecil might, I think, be used as a symbol for the way in which many of us have lost touch with nature. We have become room-bound creatures, unfamiliar with the great outdoors. We are much more comfortable sitting at home watching some natural history programme on our TV sets than we would be in the *actual* environment which is being thus portrayed.

As the memorably named Jerry Mander put it in his *Four Arguments for the Elimination of Television*, 'we find ourselves inside a kind of nationwide room, we look around it and see only our own creation'.[2] Indeed such has been the influence of television on modern life that it has sometimes been referred to as the 'first curriculum', a glittering artificial reality which claims hours of our time and attention and appears to constitute a more fundamental medium of experience and learning in the lives of some children than does the natural outdoors world. Of course TV is not the only cause of the increased interiorization of human existence, although it is undoubtedly an important factor. Looking at the way in which electricity has transformed the world, by bringing many of our activities inside, Mander remarks how, 'in the three generations since Edison, we have become creatures of light alone'.[3]

Certainly the picture of education which many people must have today is likely to be one which would correspond fairly closely to the setting in which Lucy Honeychurch puts Cecil—always indoors, in a classroom with little or no view of any note and, as likely as not, with the ever-present hum of fluorescent lights. Whereas, in years past, the 'nature ramble' around a school's grounds might have provided some on-the-spot practical work to supplement classroom teaching, comparatively few schools today boast more than a wasteland of concrete, gravel or strictly uni-functional playing fields. Indeed the grimness of many school environments provides poignant emphasis to Mike Weaver's observation that, in a depressingly urban world, the sanctity of nature may be our last moral refuge.[4] If that is indeed true, it is a refuge that many pupils may fail to find. Of course there are field trips—and films can offer a beguiling view of many of nature's miracles—but this remaining (in some cases near vestigial) contact with wilderness is, increasingly, infrequent and often unsatisfactorily second-hand. Our retreat indoors has, I would suggest, some very worrying implications.

No matter where we happen to live, what stratum of society and wealth we are born and raised in, what school we go to, what political party is in power, the fact remains that the original, primal curriculum *for everyone*, regardless of age, class, sex, colour, creed, intelligence, or any other variable, is the natural world. Though we may seldom witness a sunrise or a sunset ourselves, the measure of our days is irrevocably marked out by the setting of the sun and the rising of the same. The immutable, elemental facts of being human are facts which are dictated by the 'outdoor realities' of germination, growth, and decay. Yet it is precisely such primal realities that sometimes seem to be omitted in our schemes of education. The elements of the ancients—earth, air, water, blood and fire—seem strangely alien to the compound complexities of technology. One wonders if some of the computer generation would be able to identify examples in their raw, unrefined state. They would be more at home with concrete, car fumes, coca-cola, central heating, and so on.

I do not want to advocate some sort of backwoodsman return to the great outdoors, a Luddite destruction of technology and an unquestioning embrace of all that is 'natural' as, inevitably, also good. Such 'returns to nature' are almost always more rooted in a series of romantic misapprehensions than in anything approaching good sense. However, I *do* want to suggest some reasons for thinking that the primal curriculum should be given more attention than it is commonly accorded at present.

Today we would dismiss as ignorant and superstitious anyone who made sacrifice to a river, or respectfully consulted some god or spirit of the waters before splashing across to the other bank. Education is surely all about replacing such quaint, but erroneous, beliefs with the guiding light of reason. The trouble is, that guiding light can also dazzle and lead astray. The nature reserve where I worked as warden in the mid 1970s was cut through by three rivers of differing size and character—the Main, the Millburn and the Polldoo—each running its way across the fields and forests of County Antrim to empty into Lough Neagh, Northern Ireland's giant inland sea, along whose northern coast the reserve sprawled its untidy miles of marsh and woodland. By the end of my time there I had grown, I hope not superstitious about, but rather reverent towards, the rivers (indeed, if it does not sound too mystical, towards the 'spirit of the place'). That reverence, which I like to think was an advancement in learning rather than a retrograde step towards ignorance, was, at least in part, a reaction against the behaviour of the scores of children who visited the place.

Acting as guide to school parties was an important part of the job—and they poured into the reserve at the rate of three or four coachloads per day at the height of the season in June. Although there were some impressive counter-examples, most of the coaches simply off-loaded a cargo of aimless and intermittent energy, borne by pupils whose ignorance of the natural world was astounding and whose capacity for carelessly damaging its flora and fauna seemed limitless. A major task, after such parties had left the reserve, was simply to pick up their abundant and well-scattered litter.

Invariably, much of the litter was thrown into one of the rivers, or into the Lough itself. Such behaviour seemed in its own small way to reflect something about society at large, for the coke cans and crisp packets were only the juvenile equivalent of the rusted prams, domestic refuse and automobiles which were likewise dumped into the waters wherever the Lough or its tributaries came too close to roads or human habitation. And such rubbish was itself only mimicking pollution on the grand scale, conveniently symbolized at the western boundary of the reserve where the land was cut through by a pipeline from a local factory, a kind of poisonous 'indoor' river, which simply emptied its waste into the Lough. Is it so surprising that a society which fouls its own rivers and seas so massively should produce schoolchildren who are careless of their, by comparison, quite harmless litter?

The antics of one group in particular stay in my mind years later. Their litter was prodigious and their accompanying teachers notable for encouraging them to pick wildflowers and approach within arm's-reach of a nesting swan. But it was the way they went round the nature trail which made the deepest impression. At one point I was intrigued to find a group of them clustered around one of the numbered observation points looking intently into the trees that adjoined the path and consulting the trail guides which they had picked up at the car park. 'But where are the foxes?' they asked as I approached. 'What foxes?' I inquired. 'It says here,' said their spokesman, consulting the guide, 'in this area of the reserve there are foxes, badgers, red-squirrels, sparrowhawks and all sorts of other things. Well, we've been here for ages and can't see anything.'

They were seriously perplexed. The trail guide had listed a number of species and they expected them to be there. It had not crossed their minds that a certain amount of silence, a great deal of patient waiting and some luck are essential prerequisites of seeing all but the commonest wild creatures. I explained the problem and suggested that if they proceeded with a little more stealth they might see some wildfowl when they reached the hides which were set on stilts in the shallows of the Lough.

It is important to remember that these were children from the heart of Belfast not used to being in the countryside, and that they were poorly supervised by their teachers. It would not do to make an environmental or educational crisis of mountainous dimensions out of the molehill of boredom displayed by a party of city children on a poorly organized day's outing. And yet such complete lack of understanding of, or regard for, the natural world as they displayed does seem to illustrate some of the dimensions of our indoor attitudes. No matter how sophisticated we become, our existence depends, at the end of the day, on a very few elements. If we foul nature's water, earth and air, if we treat them with careless irreverence and ignorant disrespect, we threaten the foundations on which our lives, not to mention the lives of countless other creatures, are based. Though the children involved may have been brilliant scholars, excelling in maths, English, chemistry and so on, though they may have held between them a glittering collection of exam certificates, their behaviour that day suggested that they were profoundly uneducated.

The growing awareness of environmental issues fostered by groups such as Friends of the Earth, Greenpeace, the Royal Society for the Protection of Birds, the World Wildlife Fund and a host of others (many of whom market useful educational material), is to be welcomed. It is an awareness, moreover, whose outgrowth into 'green' politics surely promises to be one of the more interesting developments in the next century's political complexion. Stressing the importance of the primal curriculum, Jonathon Porritt has drawn attention to the ill-educated attitude of most established parties towards this fundamental basis to all our lives:

> The state of the planet provides the context within which *all* politicians operate. Yet the vast majority of them remain oblivious of that context, or choose to ignore it.[5]

There are, in addition to the above-mentioned organizations, many first-rate publications which provide passionate and informed statements of the importance of the primal curriculum to virtually every aspect of our lives. Annie Dillard's *Pilgrim at Tinker Creek*, J A Baker's *The Peregrine*, Bruce Chatwin's *The Songlines* and Hugh Brody's *The Living Arctic* (to offer a personal shortlist from a very fertile field), contain enough biological, anthropological, theological, geographical, aesthetic, economic, political and historical reflections from the point of view of deep personal experience of various of nature's 'primal curricula', to provide a wealth of fascinating and stimulating material for any teacher wondering how to counter the indoor bias of the average timetable. Outdoor, or environmental, education—in the widest sense of such terms—is a truly multidisciplinary opportunity with a potential bearing on almost every other subject on the traditional curriculum.[6]

In an essay in *The Unpainted Landscape*, David Reason writes, 'Nowadays, only 12% of Scotland's surface is wooded, and without due respect and care we shall fell the future'.[7] In a world of computers, videos, nuclear weapons, stock markets, politics and so on, it is easy to forget that the fabric of time has more fundamental determinants in terms of rivers, pastures, mountains and forests. Reason (the faculty as well as the individual!) calls for an attitude to nature that

> is not just reverential, emphasising a need to show respect for nature, but [which] also aspires to accuracy. Such understanding is only to be acquired by a scrupulous attention to things as they are. Which is not so much a demand for right thinking as for right practice.[8]

If we lose sight of such 'right practice' as a fundamental goal then there is surely a risk that our educational endeavours, successful though they may be in sustaining interest, fostering marketable skills and providing information about a wide range of subjects, will still, in an important sense, have missed the point. According to that most acute observer of the inner landscape, Henri-Frédéric Amiel, 'the test of every religious, political or educational system is the man it forms'.[9] If the person formed by our present religious, political and educational policies is happy to treat rivers as waste disposal facilities then surely such policies have failed a very basic test of adequacy.

The move from right thinking to right practice has recently been stressed by the Greenpeace organization (and as a symbol of the importance of crossing the Rubicon between words and action they have named a new Greenpeace ship 'Rubicon'). A basic task of education, and one in which many subject disciplines, including religious education, can play a part, seems to me to lie in building bridges between the primal curriculum of the natural world and our everyday experience. Such bridge-building will only be effective if the fragile biosphere which allows *all* the webs of life on this planet to be spun in the first place (from aardvarks to yuppies) is seen as sustaining all the multi-various secondary curricula which claim so much of our attention. Books and other forms of mediated experience can, of course, provide important building blocks for such bridges, but they cannot act effectively in isolation from first-hand experience. Ideally, of course, the school landscape itself would offer a teaching resource here. This is an idea which has been pursued recently in various encouraging ways, although sometimes the raw material makes it virtually impossible. Hampshire County Council, for example, are running a 'Learning through Landscapes' project, whose guiding ideal is that the school landscape 'should offer a rich and sheltered environment which should contribute positively towards child development'. The main purpose of this admirable project 'is to improve the educational potential and environmental quality of over 100,000 acres of land throughout the county'. One can only applaud such efforts and hope that their example will be followed elsewhere.

Jerry Mander has argued that America is the first culture 'to have substituted secondary, mediated versions of experience for direct experience of the world',[10] a substitution in which urbanization and television played a key role and which has led to a widespread confusion as to what constitutes 'reality'. 'As humans have moved into totally artificial environments,' Mander writes, 'our direct contact with and knowledge of the planet has been snapped. Disconnected, like astronauts floating in space, we cannot know up from down or truth from fiction.'[11]

Such disconnection and its attendant disorientation, it seems to me, is the root cause of children throwing rubbish into rivers and expecting wild animals to be on show as if they were items in a supermarket; it may also explain the less trivial manifestations of such indoors-bred ignorance, which threatens the very future of life on this planet. As such, it is surely time for an element of outdoor/environmental education to be introduced into far more areas of the school timetable than is at present countenanced, and for the primal curriculum to be given the attention its significance demands. At the very least, this might lead to right thinking about the environment which we all share (which must surely be one of education's most basic tasks). More optimistically, it might lead to an increased crossing of the vital Rubicon of integrity between understanding and actual individual behaviour. As in other areas, only education can provide a reliable bridge between the two banks.

Notes

1   E M Forster, *A Room with a View*, Harmondsworth: 1974, pp 113-14. *A Room with a View* was first published in 1908.
2   Jerry Mander, *Four Arguments for the Elimination of Television*, Brighton: 1980, p 67.
3   Ibid., p 58.
4   Mike Weaver, 'The Metamorphic Tradition in Modern Photography', in *Creation, Modern Art and Nature*, Edinburgh: 1984, p 84. (Catalogue of an exhibition to inaugurate the new gallery of the Scottish National Gallery of Modern Art at Belford Road, Edinburgh.)
5   Jonathon Porritt, *Seeing Green, the Politics of Ecology Explained*, Oxford: 1984, p 25.
6   This was a point emphasized by Philip Neal, General Secretary of the National Association for Environmental Education, in an article in the *Times Educational Supplement* of 26 June 1987. Neal noted that despite the recent upsurge of interest in environmental education, it remains an area which is seldom well catered for in schools. Among the causes of such an unsatisfactory situation, he listed inadequate teacher training, the difficulty of creating an 'environmental ethic' in everyone and the 'deployment of a fleet of watertight subjects' in many schools, an educational tactic guaranteed to frustrate any cross-curricular endeavour.
7   David Reason, 'A Hard Singing of Country', in *The Unpainted Landscape*, Edinburgh (Scottish Arts Council): 1987, p 58.
8   Ibid., p 28.
9   *Amiel's Journal, the Journal Intime of Henri-Frédéric Amiel*, translated by Mrs Humphrey Ward, London: 1913. The quotation is taken from an entry made by Amiel in Geneva on 17 June 1852.
10 Jerry Mander, op. cit., p 24. A similar view is expressed in Daniel J Boorstin's *The Image, or What Happened to the American Dream*, London: 1961.
11 Mander, ibid., p 351.

7

Shrouded in Certainty

With the recent announcement that radioactive carbon-14 dating shows the Shroud of Turin to be from the Middle Ages, many people now dismiss it as a fake. Whatever the Shroud may be, it certainly cannot be the burial shroud of Jesus. In order to qualify for *that* possibility it would, obviously, need to date from the first century. But regardless of its age, no matter how it was made, or why, I believe that the Shroud remains an extremely important resource for teachers of religious education. Its enormous *educational* potential remains unaltered, despite the fact that its *religious* significance has been so dramatically changed by the results of the carbon-14 tests. It would be a shame to see the use of the Shroud in the religious education classroom being abandoned simply because science has now shown that it is not 'genuine' in the way that many believers hoped it would be. Indeed, were its use to be abandoned on these grounds, it would only serve to confirm fears that religious education has, despite all its protestations, a covert theological agenda in favour of promoting Christian belief.

What exactly is the Shroud of Turin and why is it educationally useful?[1] At one level, at least, it is easy enough to say what the Shroud is—a band of linen, measuring some 14 feet by 3½ feet, on which is imprinted the double image (front and rear views) of a man's naked body. The image shows a bearded, long-haired man who was about 175 pounds in weight, 6 feet tall and right-handed. It was only when it was photographed, however, that the details of the faint image on the shroud emerged with any clarity, for one of the most intriguing things about the image is that it is best seen in negative. This is perhaps particularly true of the face, which emerges in a strong and haunting way. A study of the negatives from photographs of the Shroud would suggest that the man depicted here met his death by crucifixion, but reliable documentary evidence allows us to trace the Shroud back only as far as 1354, to the village of Lirey in France, from where it eventually made its way to the ownership of the Savoy family and to Turin. In the centuries since then it has been the focus of intense devotion, inquiry and controversy. Many viewed it as the burial cloth of Jesus in which his body was wrapped after it was taken from the cross, the mysterious image standing witness to his resurrection. Others, from mediaeval times onwards, have queried the authenticity of this interpretation.

With the uncertainty about the Shroud's history prior to 1354, it was crucial to try to find some reliable means of assessing its age. If it dated from the first century then it *might* be the burial shroud of Jesus; if not, then the question was settled. In 1988 the results of the carbon-14 dating of tiny pieces taken from the Shroud were announced by the laboratories in America, England and Switzerland which had been entrusted with this work. According to their tests, the Shroud dates from the Middle Ages. It cannot, therefore, be the burial shroud of Jesus.

From the point of view of the religious education teacher, the value of the Shroud does not depend on whether it happens to constitute some sort of proof for the life, death and resurrection of Jesus and the accuracy, or otherwise, of the gospel accounts of these events. Its primary importance lies in the way in which it provides an object exercise in assessing evidence, in learning how to draw valid conclusions which are adequately supported by the available facts. Regardless of what it may or may not be used as proof for, looking at the Shroud can help enormously in making clear what counts as proof. In addition to its potential for advancing learning about evidence and proof, the Shroud also provides a subject area which can be approached via several different disciplines, emphasizing the cross-curricular nature of religious education; and it can be used to introduce pupils to a fascinating subject area within religious studies, namely the whole topic of relics.

One of my recurring nightmares is of being wrongly accused of some serious crime and finding myself tried by a jury whose powers of discrimination have not developed beyond that of some of the S2 pupils with whom I have examined the Shroud. Provided only with the evidence that the Shroud shows the image of a crucified man, some will leap to the conclusion that it *must* be the image of Jesus. It is difficult to tell whether such a verdict is reached because it is what they *want* to believe, or because they think that this is the 'right answer' which is being sought, or if it is simply a case of leaping to an unsubstantiated conclusion through inattention or incomprehension. After all, even if the carbon-14 dating *had* shown that the Shroud was from the first century, this would still not prove that it was the shroud of Jesus (still less would it constitute proof of the resurrection). Crucifixion was, we should remember, a common form of execution at that time—Jesus was by no means the only person to die in this particularly horrible way. Other pupils, on being confronted with the image on the Shroud, are firmly convinced that even if the Shroud *was* from the first century, and even if it *did* display all the marks consistent with the gospel accounts of the crucifixion, that this could not possibly be Jesus—on the entirely dubious grounds that the face on the Shroud does not match the image they already have for the way Jesus 'ought' to look.

'Facts', Aldous Huxley once remarked, 'are ventriloquists' dummies. Sitting on a wise man's knee they may be made to utter words of wisdom: elsewhere, they say nothing, or talk nonsense, or indulge in sheer diabolism'.[2] One of the fundamental tasks of education must surely be to make those in its charge adept at recognizing just where the voice is coming from, and how reliable it is, when facts are said to support a certain conclusion. When someone's outlook is shrouded in unexamined certainties, there is a particular need to make them think about the nature of evidence and the circumstances under which something may be regarded as being proven beyond reasonable doubt. This is especially important when the certainties in question are attached to emotive areas like religion or politics, where the tendency towards prejudice (that is, arriving at a judgment before listening to the evidence) may be particularly strong. Certain sorts of religious and political certainty are distinctly reminiscent of Ambrose Bierce's definition of being positive about something. Being positive, he says, is simply 'being mistaken at the top of one's voice'.[3] When the ventriloquist's dummy shouts at us we should be doubly on our guard.

The Shroud is an excellent case study by means of which pupils can be introduced to the skills of handling a variety of evidence and be encouraged to formulate conclusions which are backed up by the facts (something which, scientific age or not, many of them seem unable to do with much confidence). That much of the evidence comes from disciplines other than religious education helps to emphasize the cross curricular nature of this subject. Some historical detective work is, for instance, necessary if the Shroud is to be studied properly, and so much the better if this can contain something about the conditions under which a historian will accept that something is an accurate account of the way things were. Without some basic geographical literacy, pupils will be unable to follow hypothetical reconstructions of the Shroud's travels. Since the Shroud has been subjected to pollen analysis, the biologist may be called in to comment. Can we legitimately claim, as Max Frei has done, that since it contains pollen grains from plants found only in the Holy Land, the Shroud has, indeed, been in Palestine? Or is the absence of any olive pollen proof that it could not have been in this important olive-growing area? Can pollen grains be accurately identified down to a single species of plant, or is the technique only reliable at placing specimen grains into a broad botanical genus? Chemists too can offer expert commentary on how the image on the Shroud might have been made: could it have been as a result of chemical changes on the linen fibres brought about by a mixture of the urea in a man's sweat coupled with some of the ingredients used to anoint a corpse, or is some other explanation more plausible? Photography, textile analysis, forensic science and art history have also much to contribute.

The fact that the carbon-14 dating places the Shroud in the Middle Ages provides an opportunity to study the fascinating subject of relics and to consider how and why relics have been treated so differently in different religious traditions.[4] Whilst their veneration flourished in Catholicism and Buddhism, it is rare in Protestantism, Hinduism, Islam and Judaism. This can tell us a lot about the respective theologies of the traditions concerned. More than one scholar has described the veneration of relics as the true religion of the Christian Middle Ages, so popular had the practice then become. For churches, monasteries and other places of pilgrimage, especially in Europe, possession of some crowd-pulling relic was *de rigueur*. Quite apart from any devotional importance which such relics might have, they were important sources of income. Some of the relics are somewhat surprising. There were so many vials of the Virgin's breast milk in countless churches throughout Christendom that John Calvin was led to remark that even had she been a cow she could not have produced so much! No fewer than seven churches claimed to possess Jesus' circumcised foreskin, and there was so much wood from the True Cross that Calvin doubted whether three hundred men, let alone one, could have carried it. But if some of the relics are surprising, the fact that a trade in false and fraudulent relics grew up is not (after all, with Louis IX of France finding that his offer of 15,000 florins for the bones of Thomas Aquinas was not enough to secure them, it is clear that relics had a commercial value over and above any religious one). Is it possible that the Shroud might have been faked for financial gain (after all, it was put on show in Lirey in the 1350s precisely in order to supplement the income of an impoverished noble-woman)?

Such a theory is not without problems. If the Shroud does indeed date from the Middle Ages, as the scientists now tell us, how are we to explain the fact that some paintings from the fifth and sixth centuries seem to base their depiction of Christ on the image which is borne on the Shroud? How, if it was the work of a mediaeval relic-monger, did he know to put the nail wounds in the wrists, rather than in the palms of the hands (as was the dominant artistic tradition at that time)? After all, it was not until 1968 that archaeological finds confirmed how the victim of this gruesome form of execution was pinned by nails driven through the wrists. How, even more perplexingly, did any mediaeval maker of the Shroud know that when a nail is driven through the wrists the median nerve snaps, causing the thumbs to move inwards across the palms, in exactly the way they feature on the Shroud? And how did the image actually get on the cloth? There is no trace of paint on the Shroud; the image is created by the partial breakdown of the cellulose fibres in the linen. How could such an image be manufactured? Despite many scientific certainties about it, the Shroud remains something of a mystery. No matter what it turns out to be, it is a teaching aid *par excellence* for the religious education class. It fascinates and holds the attention of almost all age ranges with a mixture of the bizarre, the mysterious, the improbable and the gruesome (a study of it is guaranteed, at the very least, to dispel any cosmetic notions about what crucifixion involved).

At a time when 'active citizenship' and individual responsibility are watchwords of the government's philosophy, one would hope that a subject which can make so substantial a contribution to an understanding of evidence, proof and reaching reasonable conclusions, will be seen as central to the curriculum. In some respects at least, its endeavours constitute nothing less than a kind of propaedeutics of civic responsibility. After all, if a democracy is to survive, its electorate must be equipped with the skills and information necessary to make sound choices. Such responsible choices would be impossible without an ability to acquire and handle the evidence that is relevant to reaching decisions about any particular matter, which is precisely one of the skills which religious education fosters (and fosters in an area which tends all too frequently towards intolerance, bigotry and a refusal to look honestly at the facts).

If it seems to some that the carbon-14 testing of the Shroud of Turin has delivered a blow to faith which they would prefer not to have happened, it is worth stressing that such findings do nothing to affect its significant educational potential (a consideration which must surely have some religious value too?). It is perhaps also worth remembering that, in matters religious, certainty may not always be what it seems. As Miguel de Unamuno put it:

Whoever believes he believes in God, but believes without passion, without anguish, without uncertainty, without doubt, without despair-in-consolation, believes only in the God-idea, not in God Himself.[5]

Notes

1   There is a wealth of literature on the Shroud. I base the account I give here on Ian Wilson's *The Turin Shroud*, London: 1978.

2   Aldous Huxley, *Time Must Have a Stop*, London: 1945, p 295.

3   Ambrose Bierce, *The Devil's Dictionary*. There have been many editions of this entertaining volume, which was first published in the 1880s. I am quoting from *The Enlarged Devil's Dictionary*, edited by Ernest Jerome Hopkins and published by Penguin in 1971.

4   The information on relics in this chapter is taken from the excellent article by John S Strong in volume 12 (pp 275-82) of the *Encyclopedia of Religion*, general editor Mircea Eliade, New York: 1987.

5   Miguel de Unamuno, *The Tragic Sense of Life in Men and Nations*, Anthony Kerrigan (tr), London: 1972, p 211.

8

Dancing Class

Perhaps one of the most unfortunate attributes of the species *Homo sapiens* is our tendency to condemn what is different as mistaken, inferior or threatening. Some of the more serious consequences of this trait have been explored by Sam Keen in his fascinating study of the psychology of enmity. Focussing on the art and literature of propaganda, Keen shows how the hostile imagination often begins with the simple assumption that 'what is strange or unknown is dangerous and intends us evil'.[1] From such a premise can develop the process of dehumanizing others, presenting them as faceless automatons, or as animals or monsters, which can in turn lead to persecution, war and even genocide. If we add to this tendency of condemning what is different our less than perfect powers of observation, its already considerable potential for destruction is significantly compounded. One of the basic tasks of education, it seems to me, must be to foster a spirit of honest inquiry, based on accurate observation, which can act as a first line of defence against our leaping to unfounded conclusions—conclusions which can have such serious implications for our relationships with those of other religions, races and nations.

This is, perhaps, little more than a long-winded way of stating the obvious, namely that education must do battle with prejudice, our readiness to pronounce a verdict before (*prae*) the evidence has been heard and a judgment (*judicium*) fairly reached. This battle is of particular importance in *religious* education, where we are dealing with an area of human experience which seems to be extremely susceptible to the mis-perceptions of prejudice, and where the outcome of such mis-perceptions often results in particularly barbarous behaviour towards our fellows. Keen's study, for example, contains many references to the religious factors used in those excesses of our unreasoning hostility towards those who happen to be different from us. Such hostility is almost invariably based on prejudice, rather than on accurate observation and considered judgment. I want to begin by showing that 'seeing what is really there' is not so straightforward as it may sound,

47

The Shiva Nataraja

before moving on to consider a specific example, in the image of the dancing Shiva (see page 48), of how the religious educator might take steps towards schooling our powers of observation and curbing our impulse to condemn the unfamiliar out of hand before we have had a chance to look at it carefully and see what it means.

It is difficult to believe that we sometimes cannot see what is there in front of us, yet there is disturbing evidence for just such a blind-spot in the way human beings look at the world. Consider, for example, the outcome of that somewhat unethical (but nonetheless instructive) experiment where a fake murder attempt is staged on a lecturer (with his connivance) mid-way through one of his classes. Although his would-be assailant has been in full view of the unsuspecting students for several minutes, their subsequent descriptions of him, as Arne Trankell has shown in his work on witness reliability, are likely to be vague and inaccurate.[2] Of course in one sense the students in such a situation quite clearly saw the 'murderer'; in another sense, however, apparently they did not. As the naturalist J A Baker put it, after ten years devoted to watching one of Britain's most beautiful and elusive birds of prey, the Peregrine Falcon, 'the hardest thing of all is to see what is really there'.[3] His comments would seem to hold true over a much wider range of human activity than that which falls only within the ornithologist's field of interest.

Sometimes our failure to see what is there simply involves straightforward factors which would immediately affect any attempt at accurate observation. If the situation is one in which we are startled or frightened, for example, it will clearly not be conducive to the sort of studied looking that calmer surroundings allow. Often, however, it is more a question of our expectations and presuppositions preventing us from seeing what is actually there before us. In *Much Maligned Monsters*, for example, a book which charts the fascinating history of Western reactions to Indian art, Partha Mitter stresses the extent to which cultural presuppositions colour the way we perceive things. Thus the first European travellers to India described the pantheon of gods they found there in terms which had very little connection with what was really there. As Mitter puts it, the early travellers 'preferred to trust what they had been taught to expect instead of trusting their own eyes'.[4] Reading their accounts and looking at the illustrations which appear in works like Varthemas's *Itinerario*, first published in 1510, it is difficult to tell with any certainty what those early pioneers actually saw. Clearly in one sense they encountered exactly the same temples and sculptures as the Indians themselves saw (many of which still survive today); but in another 'seeing', as Mitter shows, they saw instead all the monsters and devils which two powerful traditions in the intellectual milieu of the European Middle Ages predisposed them to see. The tradition established in secular literature regarding the East as a veritable font of monsters and marvels (a tradition taken over from Classical sources), and the tradition of demonology which was firmly established in the religious literature of the time, both exerted a potent influence.

The extent to which expectations can colour actuality is remarkable. Another striking example of this is recorded by Jonathan Spence in his brilliant study of the Jesuit missionary Matteo Ricci, who visited India en route to China, where he lived from 1583 until his death in 1610. Spence notes how the first Portuguese navigators to reach South India actually worshipped before images of the goddess Kali, because they believed her to be the Virgin Mary. This identification of Kali with the Virgin presumably took place very largely because of what they believed about the existence of indigenous Christians in India—'St Thomas Christians' or 'Malabar Christians', as they were known at the time.[5] But, given that Kali is almost invariably portrayed in the most lurid terms as a savage, demonic, bloodthirsty figure, wearing a necklace of skulls or severed human heads, wielding a sword and often dancing on a prostrate body, this particular instance of mistaken identity suggests a quite remarkable failure of observation and a consequent leaping to conclusions which, on closer examination, would be seen not to follow. We have a great facility for seeing what we expect (or what we want) to see.

It is easy to be patronisingly amused by the way in which our ancestors leapt to the wrong conclusions about each other's beliefs and customs—history is full of entertaining examples (as well as those more sombre ones which have led to widespread persecution and cruelty). But are we that much more enlightened? Even the most cursory glance at current affairs would suggest that, particularly where religion is involved, prejudice rather than patience, blindness rather than informed insightfulness, often characterize the way in which we treat the beliefs of others. We see what we expect to see, and all too often our expectations are imbued with suspicion, condemnation and hostility.

The extent to which presuppositions can determine what we actually see is, increasingly, being recognized as a human attribute of great significance, not only in social but also in scientific terms. Considerable doubt has now been cast on the picture of the scientist as a wholly objective impersonal figure proceeding along a straight road of unswerving rationality, towards a goal whose attainment has nothing to do with extraneous subjective factors. In his classic study of, and entitled, *The Structure of Scientific Revolutions*, for example, Thomas Kuhn has drawn attention to the way in which scientists, like the rest of us, view the world according to socially sanctioned 'paradigms'. Anything which does not fall into line with the paradigm which happens to be dominant at any particular time, is difficult to see as such. It simply tends to be assimilated into the familiar picture, whether it 'really' fits into it or not.

A neat illustration of this tendency occurs in the experiment of the anomalous cards which is cited by Kuhn.[6] In this experiment, 'anomalous' cards, such as a black four of hearts, were introduced into a normal pack. But when the pack was dealt through to an observer, he/she almost invariably failed to identify these 'rogue' elements. Instead, the anomalous cards were perceived as normal. They were, as Kuhn puts it, 'immediately fitted to one of the conceptual categories prepared by prior experience without any awareness of trouble'.[7] 'Seeing is believing' is a saying which seems to have an important vice-versa sense as well. Perhaps along with word-blindness and colour-blindness we should consider the possible existence of something not unlike 'transcendence-blindness', for if it is difficult for us to see anomalous cards, think how much more difficult it may be to notice something as radically unlike our other experience as the holy.[8]

The Shiva Nataraja is widely regarded as one of the triumphs of Hindu art, blending in a single symbol a wealth of religious vision with an essential simplicity of form. Its aesthetic merits have not gone unnoticed in the West, where no less an authority than Rodin has praised its beauty.[9] Titus Burckhardt suggests that it is perhaps 'the most perfect fruit of Hindu art',[10] and its potency as a religious symbol has moved that great commentator on Eastern art and philosophy, Heinrich Zimmer, to write some of his most lyrical passages in explication of what the image means.[11] The image depicts Shiva (whom R C Zaehner has dubbed 'the most numinous and disturbing representation of deity that Hinduism was to produce'[12]) as Lord of the Dance, and provides an excellent case study of how religious education can offer much needed training in seeing what is really there, instead of leaping to conclusions about what we think we see, or what we have decided *a priori* to make of other people's beliefs or the forms in which they find expression.

I have used the Shiva Nataraja with a range of classes at school level, with undergraduate students of comparative religion, and with mature students attending various summer schools. Across a wide range of age, interest and ability, the Lord of the Dance offers a means of advancing learning in a variety of ways. None of them, to my mind, is as important as the way in which a study of it can train the observation and tame our inclination to dismiss out of hand as silly, grotesque or wrong-headed what appears so different from the artistic and religious forms we have grown accustomed to.

A class's first impressions of the Shiva Nataraja will invariably yield some interesting off-the-cuff reactions, ranging from the unthinking Philistine rejection of the strange, through the interested questioning of something puzzlingly unfamiliar, to that instantly appreciative feeling for great art which seems to transcend age, race and language. Any class I have asked to write a brief description of the image, after carefully studying it for only three or four minutes, has provided repeated illustration of how difficult it is to see what is really there, especially when what we see is something novel and unexpected. Almost every class, when prompted towards a more studied observation, has made me look again at what I assumed I had seen quite adequately already.

It is more instructive to see the Nataraja image as a graphic illustration of the Hindu worldview, as a kind of theological diagram, rather than as an *objet d'art* designed merely to please the eye. Just how far one decides to let the image take the observer into that worldview will, of course, depend on the class and the time at the teacher's disposal. However far we may go, the Shiva Nataraja offers access to a fascinating outlook on the world—at least to those who can see beyond the 'No Entry' of initial dissimilarity and foreignness.

Even the most basic aspects of the image can by-pass the stare of hostile dismissal. That the god is depicted with four arms is not, for example, as readily apparent as we might suppose, and needs to be pointed out to some observers. These multiple arms together denote power and, taken singly, each one expands on this general theme. Shiva's upper right hand holds a drum (shaped like an hourglass) on which he beats out, in the rhythm of the dance, the rhythm of life and death. His upper left hand bears on its open palm a naked flame, testimony to the god's destructive potential and to the discipline with which that potential is managed. The lower right hand is held in the 'fear not' gesture, inviting humankind to approach without dread what may seem awesome and terrifying. The lower left hand points to the god's dancing feet, where, at the base of the image, lies the prostrate figure of the demon Apasmara, whose name means 'ignorance' and on whose back Shiva dances, preventing him from rising. Shiva dances within an encircling hoop. This is the prabhamandala, a ring of flames and light which represents the vital processes of the universe and all its creatures; it is the flickering dance of nature sustained by the god at centre, from whom floods the energy which ignites, extinguishes and rekindles all the various flames of life (Ananda Coomaraswamy has described the Nataraja as 'an image of that energy which science must postulate behind all phenomena'[13]). Shiva's assymetrical earrings denote that he (and of course 'he' is a misnomer in this context) is both male and female, this androgyny sometimes being further emphasized by a single female breast. The significance of these androgynous features lies in the way in which they show how this concept of God belongs to a conceptual category outwith the simple sexual dualism of our vocabulary. Moreover, Shiva's indeterminate dual gender reflects a more general ambivalence which is a centrally important theme recurring throughout the rich mythology associated with this deity.

This is just to *begin* to unravel some of the symbolism found in the image. The crescent moon, the miniature figure of the goddess Ganga, the skull and flowers in Shiva's unshorn hair, the god's third eye and the cobra twined around one wrist, the lotus on which the demon Apasmara lies, the trailing scarf—all these add further nuances of meaning to the symbol of which they form a part. My intention here, however, is not to provide an exhaustive commentary, but simply to indicate how the Nataraja image may be of educational use in training us to make a better stab at seeing what is really there, when we are confronted with something from a religious and cultural background quite different from our own.

There are, of course, those who would question the wisdom of introducing so foreign and complex a symbol into the classroom and expecting schoolchildren to be anything but perplexed by it. Whilst I would share their concern that pupils ought not to be exposed too soon to concepts whose understanding presupposes a certain level of maturity, I would argue that an image such as that of the Shiva Nataraja can be approached on a variety of levels so as to suit the interests and aptitudes of any particular class. The important thing, it seems to me, is to bring such 'outlandish' things into the classroom at the earliest opportunity, so that pupils may be taught that first appearances are often incomplete and inaccurate and that even what may strike them to begin with as weird and perplexing will yield intelligible meaning if careful observation and reflection are applied to it. Only if reason 'fears not' and patiently approaches what may be strange and off-putting, without resort to the easy dismissals of prejudice, can we hope to make much progress in what Max Müller called 'the great art of human life'[14] —namely, learning to understand each other (which is presumably one of religious education's fundamental desiderata). Both in terms of providing the raw material for a simple exercise in accurate observation, and in showing the depth of meaning which a symbol can hold, the Shiva Nataraja is of considerable educational potential. Furthermore, it invites the sort of multi-disciplinary approach which is appropriate to religious education as a cross-curricular exercise whose concerns cannot adequately be addressed if they are confined within strict subject boundaries.

The image of the Shiva Nataraja offers a full-scale lesson in the observation and interpretation of symbols, and introduces to the present-day observer a religious concept thought to date from around 2000 BC (showing how meaning may still be found in what is distant from us in time and place). The interpretation of the Nataraja's symbolism leads on naturally to the stories in the profuse and colourful mythology which has grown up around this deity. The fact that Shiva is *dancing* invites a look at the importance of dance as a means of religious expression, and can also provide an opportunity to listen to Indian music. The name of the process by which the images were traditionally made, the so called '*cire perdue*' (or lost wax) method, can provide a starting point for a consideration of the ways in which artists and craftsmen can put their skill to use in expressing abstract ideas. The fact that Shiva is portrayed in human form, but is clearly assumed to have suprahuman powers, cautions against literal anthropomorphic interpretation in the sphere of religious symbolism. The ambiguity of the god ('he' is both male and female, creator and destroyer, ascetic and erotic) offers a reminder concerning the difficulty of expressing religious concepts in words and, in consequence, of the special uses of language which are employed in this whole area of human experience. There are, in short, *many* lessons to be learned from the dancing Shiva, lessons in which history, art, literature and music can all play a part. Of course this should come as no surprise, for religious education is, after all (or it certainly ought to be), an integrating as well as integral part of the curriculum.

'A great motif in religion or art, any great symbol', according to Ananda Coomaraswamy, 'becomes all things to all men'.[15] To let this fecundity of meaning blossom, however, we must first learn to see what is there. As the communications revolution renders the diverse societies of humankind into one inter-conscious world, bringing many 'strange' phenomena to our attention, and as our own culture becomes increasingly pluralistic, it is surely time to widen our religious and aesthetic vocabulary so that it is not constrained by the terms of any single tradition. If we are to rid ourselves of the dangers of ethnocentrism,[16] we must make sure that education helps us to see and appreciate the meaning of the kind of religious symbols which our ancestors dismissed as demonic or monstrous, and which many of our contemporaries often seem similarly inclined to disparage (for the untutored imagination still tends toward the hostile and xenophobic if left to its own devices).

The Shiva Nataraja image provides a highly specific (and, I hope, an encouraging) example of the sort of practical, positive contribution which religious education can make to our society, through its insistence that 'other' forms of faith, like our own, need to be carefully and patiently observed before judgments are ventured about them. We surely do not need to look too long at the prejudicial consequences of *not* bothering to see what is there in the religious realm, to appreciate what a crucially important subject this is.

Notes

1   Sam Keen, *Faces of the Enemy*, San Francisco: 1986, p 18.

2   Arne Trankell, *Reliability of Evidence*, Stockholm: 1972, pp 33-45.

3   J A Baker, *The Peregrine*, London: 1967, p 19. Baker also issues a caution about watching peregrines which students of religion might take to heart regarding their subject matter: 'Books about the birds show pictures. . .large and isolated in the gleaming whiteness of the page, the hawk stares back at you, bold, statuesque, brightly coloured. But when you have shut the book, you will never see that bird again' (ibid). There tends to be a similar gulf between religion as presented in books and the faith which can be observed in the lives of its contemporary representatives.

4   Partha Mitter, *Much Maligned Monsters, A History of European Reactions to Indian Art*, Oxford: 1977, p 2.

5   Jonathan D Spence, *The Memory Palace of Matteo Ricci*, London: 1985, pp 111-12.

6   Thomas S Kuhn, *The Structure of Scientific Revolutions*, second (enlarged) edition, Chicago: 1970, p 63.

7   Ibid.

8   Perhaps such 'transcendence blindness' might help to explain what Edward Robinson (in *The Language of Mystery*, London: 1987, p 81) dubs the 'Acquired Immunity to Mystery Syndrome', a phenomenon with which every teacher of religious education must surely be familiar. On the highly 'anomalous' nature of the holy, see my 'Ineffability and Intelligibility: Towards an Understanding of the Radical Unlikeness of Religious Experience', *International Journal for Philosophy of Religion*, vol 20 (1986), pp 109-29.

9   *Ars Asiatica*, vol III (1921), pp 9-13.

10   Titus Burckhardt, *Sacred Art in East and West*, Lord Northbourne (tr), Middlesex: 1967, p 38.

11   See Heinrich Zimmer, *Myths and Symbols in Indian Art and Civilization*, New York: 1946, pp 151, 174, and *The Art of Indian Asia*, New York: 1955, pp 122-4

12   R C Zaehner, *Hinduism*, Oxford: 1962, p 33.

13   Ananda Coomaraswamy, *The Dance of Shiva, Fourteen Indian Essays*, New Delhi: 1976, p 78.

14   Friedrich Max Müller, *The Silesian Horseherd*, Oscar Fechter (tr), London: 1903, p 216.

15   Coomaraswamy, op. cit., p 67.

16   In condemning ethnocentrism one would do well to consider Allan Bloom's thought-provoking comments in his important book *The Closing of the American Mind* (New York: 1987). For instance, on p 34 he argues that condemning ethnocentrism can, in fact, involve the assertion of the superiority of a scientific understanding and the inferiority of cultures which do not follow such a methodology. Much of Bloom's book (subtitled 'How Higher Education has Failed Democracy and Impoverished the Souls of Today's Students') has profound implications for many of the central assumptions of modern religious education.

Part II

Shooting Round Corners:
Essay by Analogy

In *Sense and Sensibilia*, the philosopher J L Austin describes the word 'like' as being a 'flexibility device' in language which allows us to shoot round corners and avoid being left speechless when our limited vocabulary fails.[1] By extension, I would suggest that analogy can sometimes help us to see aspects of a subject which, if dealt with more directly, might be missed. These 'essays by analogy' attempt to cast light on religious education by using analogical images (Tunnels, Skulls, Tigers, and suchlike). Although some readers may find this an oblique and confusing way to proceed, I hope that by way of such images we can avoid a slavishly uncritical acceptance of those straight lines of thought which tradition sometimes imposes at the expense of intellectual flexibility. Most of these essays have already appeared in print in some form (again, mostly in the Scottish edition of the *Times Educational Supplement*), but appear here with the appropriate revisions.

1   J L Austin, *Sense and Sensibilia*, reconstructed from the manuscript notes by G J Warnock, Oxford: 1962, p 74f.

9

Tunnels, Skulls and High-risk Homework

What, on the school timetable, is boring, a waste of time, irrelevant, a load of rubbish or, in a word, crap? The comments are culled from pupils' scribbles, mutters and heartfelt airings of opinion about religious education, and it is a rare teacher of the subject who has not encountered a substantial barrage of such disheartening feedback.

I suppose the fortunate religious education teacher eventually reaches a state of professional enlightenment which is no longer surprised or depressed by the low opinion with which the subject is commonly regarded, but remains simply determined to work steadily against the misconceptions behind its widespread rejection in the closed minds of pupils, parents and staff alike. The less fortunate are doubtless fated to become denizens of disillusionment's various dark abodes—idealism turned to drudgery, cynicism, despair and other such sad milestones along the gauntlet of perils with which, like most others, this particular road to enlightenment is lined.

Still at that undespairing stage of being shocked into words (rather than stunned into silence) by the glaring incongruity between the actual status of religious education and its real value, I write this beginner's view in the hope that when I encounter moments of disillusionment on the road ahead I may look back and see some light at the beginning of the tunnel even though none is visible ahead.

In fact the idea of a tunnel provides a surprisingly apt image for the whole endeavour of religious education. For although religion *can* be used (or rather misused) as a powerful prop for maintaining the status quo, there is a strong case to be made for arguing that the main emphasis of religion, far from shoring up our accustomed certainties, lies in an attempt to undermine and break through all those comfortable assumptions of material security which blindfold us to the precarious transience of human existence. Much of the energy of the great religious traditions is focussed into tunnelling beneath our mundane preoccupations, thus weakening such structures as career, income and possessions which we spend so much time erecting to cover an essential—and in the end uncoverable—nakedness. Only when the towering all-importance of such materialistic concerns is toppled can we seriously assess our position against more permanent markers than those afforded by the polestar of mere comfort.

It is strange how few people seem to have noticed that religion is potentially the most subversive subject to be considered on the school curriculum. Perhaps the legacy of sickly scripture lessons endured by previous generations has passed into the genetic memory and prevents so radical a departure from the remembered norm of sugared piety. Religion is subversive because an acquaintance with its perspectives on life may serve to undermine a great many of those weighty edifices which society constructs upon each individual psyche and sets such store by, edifices which hide us from ourselves and whose shadows can allow commerce to eclipse compassion, possessions to deaden pity, and luxury to dull our native sense of mystery. Beneath each variety of materialistic blindness there is a tunnel of religious sight. Religious education shows us that these tunnels exist and takes us some little way down them on a guided tour. Since that knowledge is almost bound to make us less certain than we were before, regardless of how we react to it, the subject, as well as the subject matter it deals with, must be considered as having a distinctly disruptive side. Religious education holds up the mirror of religion (or rather the mirrors of religion), so that alongside our customary reflections we encounter the stranger within our own images. Should the means of conveying such vital self-knowledge be given so small a share of the school timetable?

Mirrors (as we shall see later in more detail) can provide a second useful image to help clarify the nature of religious education. Whereas earlier generations in this country stood before a single religious reflection of the world, which provided a stolidly singular Christian image, our own generation has left behind so relatively straightforward a religious context and finds itself surrounded by a veritable *hall* of mirrors showing Christian, Hindu, Jewish, Buddhist and Islamic images of ourselves. Each one presents a challenge to our sense of mundane identity and everyday appearance and, cumulatively, the religious images place an instant question mark against the sufficiency of any non-religious view. Religious education presents (or ought to present) the differing reflections clearly and offers some comment on how to understand what we see glittering before us. By making us aware of the existence of so many possible religious identities, it is almost bound to leave us less certain of who we are than we were before we took its guided tour of human religiousness. Can we afford to rush such a journey?

What, then, is religion, and what is religious education that they can be likened to tunnels and mirrors? Are such comparisons useful or do they simply sacrifice accuracy for eye-catching phrases? Any study of religion which progresses beyond the level of fatuous factuality is almost bound to loosen the knots holding up the manifold blindfolds of our everyday certainties. For a glimpse of the cavernous religious tunnels which underlie our mundane shallowness will almost certainly send a shiver of uncertainty, if not terror, through those attitudes of bored and complacent ignorance which dismiss this whole area of profoundly exciting—although disturbing—human experience as irrelevant. After all, can we seriously hope to return quite comfortably to a single-minded pursuit of executive status, high income, house, car and holiday—or whatever other secular grails happen to be in vogue—after reading the Upanishads, the New Testament, the Qur'an, the Dhammapada and other great religious texts and considering those questions of morality, eschatology and metaphysics which they bring to our attention? Although such questions may, in the end, be unanswerable, is it wise simply to ignore them?

In very broad terms, religious education is an effort to provide people with the information and skills appropriate to their dealing competently with religious issues (issues which centre around the question of life's meaning). It is *not* an evangelical activity, it is *not* just Bible study, it does *not* presuppose or even encourage belief in God. If departmental allocations allowed it, standard classroom equipment might include a human skull—some such *memento mori* being necessary if the informational side of the subject is not to be a facile list of names and dates; and were it possible to arrange, religious education homework might usefully consist of instructions to go alone some stormy night to a wild and empty place, and there, gazing up at the infinitude of space, to think about the loneliness of being a mere pinprick of sentience. For if the skills which are taught are to extend beyond looking up Biblical quotations and spelling transliterated Sanskrit words correctly, then surely some familiarity at least with our finitude, if not with the numinous, should be actively encouraged.

And what, I hear you ask, is the point of looking in mirrors which provide disturbing (if not downright terrifying) pictures? What is the point of exploring tunnels which burrow dangerously beneath all the comfortable assumptions which provide some sense of security? Why ought we to countenance the presence on the school curriculum of a subject which seems inevitably to lead to admitting a disruptive element into our normally contented worldview (a worldview which the rest of the school system provides much of the cement for)?

As well as being potentially the most subversive subject, religion (and by association religious education) can also justly lay claim to being potentially the most *con*structive subject to be considered on the school curriculum. And it is because its *constructive* potential is so great that the low place so frequently assigned to religious education seems quite ludicrously incongruous. Of course we may not pass beyond the subversive stage, indeed we may never reach it if religious education remains overly preoccupied with history, but can we afford not to take the risk when such a reward is offered?

That great flowering of spirituality in sixth century India, which finds expression in the Upanishads, coincided with the discovery and use of iron and the resulting increase in leisure time due to the general improvement in technology which followed. When people had time to think, their thoughts turned to the mystery of existence. It is a so-far unsubstantiated personal hypothesis that our time will see a similar blossoming of the religious dimension with the increase in leisure time brought about by micro-technology. Why has this blossoming (with such potentially beneficial consequences) not yet occurred? Perhaps one important factor here is quite simply the level of religious illiteracy in our society, caused by years of mediocre (or non-existent) religious education. Religious education cannot, and ought not to try to, usurp the function of religion. It cannot fertilize spiritual sterility. It can, however, facilitate conditions where the *possibility* of such fertilization is not denied, where the religious facts of life are unblushingly made known. For those facts to be made known requires not only greater awareness of the importance of religious education, but a practical expression of such awareness in terms of staffing, timetables and the allocation of resources.

A confrontation with fear will expose mere sophistry and religiosity for the fakes they are—and who has ever passed through life without many such confrontations? As William Golding puts it, 'Philosophy and religion—what are they when the wind blows and the water gets up in lumps?'[1] The acid test of religion is just this: does its constructive side, the answers that it offers to life's yawning negativities, evaporate when the going gets rough and we are faced with fear and loneliness and a sense of utter futility? The acid test of religious education is surely whether it has taught us to distinguish between religion and religiosity, in ourselves and in others, before the acid bites. And if its educative process seems to leave us more vulnerable to the acid's anticipated sting, then surely rather than abandoning religious education as dangerously subversive we ought to welcome the perspective it offers, for false security is no security at all, and comfort gained in ignorance of the probing, questioning tunnels and mirrors of humankind's age-old spirituality is likely to be short-lived.

It is important to keep in mind throughout the distinction between religion and religious education. The acid test for one ought not to be transferred to the other. If, as Wittgenstein suggests, 'to pray is to think about the meaning of life',[2] then religion and education *do* have many important points of overlap. But it would surely be quite mistaken to go much further in conflating them than making such a broad identification of general aims. To go further almost invariably leads from education to evangelism or from spirituality to scholasticism.

Compared to the chalk-face flying hours clocked up by some of my colleagues I am scarcely more than a fledgling. I have fluttered enough in the classroom, though, to anticipate the unease which they will feel at these general statements, these colourful abstract pronouncements. What, the gruff voice of experience asks, is the relevance of all this to the classroom? It has something to do with looking far enough behind and ahead not to get bogged down in the present, a kind of Green Cross Code that looks beyond the oncoming traffic for a *reason* to cross over. Day to day classroom survival is, obviously, a prerequisite for achieving anything, but if it is bought at the expense of mindlessly crossing roads just to get to the other side of a day, a week, a term, then surely it is time to stand still on the kerbside of the subject and think where we are trying to get to.

And where *have* we got to? I can only give a provisional and personal assessment, for doubtless different teachers reach different destinations at different times. On bad days, worried by some further darkening of the ever-lengthening shadow of the bomb, ravaged by the mindless baiting of my worst S2 class, and pigeon-holed unmercifully as a religious education teacher and therefore piously narrow-minded, ineffectual, prim and prudish by some new acquaintance, religious education seems like a lost cause. On good days, inspired by news of someone really working for the common good, amazed by some flash of pupil insight and asked profoundly intelligent questions about religious issues by quite unexpected people, it seems more akin to the white dove of hope which escaped from Pandora's box along with all the world's misfortunes.

Doubtless such oscillations between extremes will level out as I become fully fledged in my craft. If my thinking on the subject ever levels out to some dull straight line, though, I hope I will still have sense enough to realize that it's time to set *myself* some high-risk homework, to go alone at night into whatever wilderness is left, and there, unaccompanied by thoughts of lesson preparation, curriculum development or global megadeath, face my own mysterious, unique and transient existence and send Wittgensteinian prayers like fireflies into the ever-present darkness.

Notes

1   William Golding, *Rites of Passage*, London: 1980, p 16.
2   Ludwig Wittgenstein, *Notebooks 1914–1916*, G E M Anscombe (tr), Oxford: 1961, entry dated 11 June 1916.

10

Some Reflections from the Hall of Mirrors

The bruise which resulted from not bending as I went through the low stone doorway of the Buddhist monastery in Northumberland, lasted for some days and provided a tangible reminder of the need to be flexible when exploring religions. Getting inside other people's beliefs and trying to see what they are all about, rather than just standing at the doorstep and judging them from external appearances alone, is a vitally important task as the multiplicity of beliefs contained in the world's religions becomes ever more a day-to-day reality and less a distant, scarcely intruding, fact of life lived elsewhere. It is not always an easy task and some bruising of preconceived ideas is almost bound to occur, but this seems a small price to pay for its eventual reward: an increased understanding of our neighbours, if not of ourselves as well.

My visit to the Buddhist monastery was in the capacity of religious adviser to 'Hall of Mirrors', a series of programmes made by Scottish Television for Channel 4.[1] The series attempted to take viewers inside the doorways of a number of religions (and certain non-religious outlooks such as Humanism and Marxism too) in order to see how they look from the point of view of the believers who live there. In terms of the background work with which I was involved, which dealt in particular with non-Christian religions, gaining entry posed certain problems, with suspicions of trespass or trivialization often having to be allayed before the door was opened more than a chink. Leave-taking too was not without its difficulties.

The religious situation in the West today can be likened to being in a hall of mirrors in the sense that we no longer stand before the single mirror of Christianity and see reflected before us, albeit in many different facets, an exclusively Christian vision of the world. Instead, we are faced with a confusing variety of images. The mirrors of Hinduism, Buddhism, Islam, Sikhism and so on suggest many seemingly different pictures of ourselves and the world we live in, and further reflections are added by the growth of various non-religious (or at least non-theistic) outlooks too.

In such a situation the question seems automatically to arise: 'Which image, if any, shows a *true* picture of who and where we are?' (and thus of what we ought to *do*, for all these reflections are chiefly concerned with one very basic matter—how we ought to live our lives). It is unlikely that we shall find any answer which does more than mirror our existing prejudices if we go no further than looking at surface reflections. The situation seems to call for entering into rather than gazing at. Doorways must be negotiated so that we can go beyond the dazzle of first impressions. Behind each mirror lies a many-roomed mansion; the programmes attempted to take the viewer some way inside. They tried to edge towards the heart of the matter so as to show what animates these different visions of life and makes their millions of adherents remain faithful to them.

Quite apart from the bruise received there, my visit to the Buddhist monastery was memorable for the quiet authority of its abbot and his readiness to communicate in simple terms what had made him abandon the civil service for a life of meditation in the wilds of Northumbria. His readiness to welcome in and open many doors for a curious stranger contrasted sharply with the attitude of one of his co-religionists further south who felt disinclined to talk with me, and promptly didn't, despite an arranged time and place of meeting and my round trip of some 1000 miles to see him. This is a lesson, perhaps, to those who might over-rate the importance of television, and a useful reminder that whether Christian, Hindu, Buddhist, Muslim or Sikh, individuals are precisely what that word implies, no matter what general heading you might seek to group them under. As I left him still seated cross-legged and seemingly imperturbable in his meditation hall, my annoyance at a wasted journey was tempered with the realization that *his* quest—for enlightenment—left mine, as a mere programme adviser, worthy of indefinite postponement.

Other thought-provoking incidents stick vividly in mind: the Hindu temple in a disused Unitarian church where the symbolism of Christianity was not discarded but was preserved and added to—indeed the shrine room contained symbols from *all* the world's great religions, evidence of Hinduism's baffling ability to absorb almost anything into its complex pantheon; talking with a Scottish-born convert to Islam, whose accent alone suggested interestingly homely perspectives on such hitherto foreign-sounding names as 'Muhammad', 'Qur'an' and 'Allah'; finding a terrace house deep in the East End of London where, amidst utterly—not to say depressingly—British surroundings, the many-armed god Shiva, one of India's greatest deities, was worshipped with colourful devotion; discussing aspects of Sikhism, Taoism and Baha'i with Glaswegians, Londoners, Liverpudlians; and receiving offers from dubious sources to come and talk about their god . . . . One thing is certain, the hall of mirrors is glittering brightly in this country even if many choose to ignore it and clutch to themselves instead some single cherished image that has long since cracked or become grimy with age and neglect. Seeing such vibrant diversity it is hard to imagine any outlook on the world—religious or otherwise—which would not benefit from a thorough re-appraisal in the face of so many apparently viable alternatives.

A few months later, after the programmes were recorded, I started work as a teacher of religious education, that surely most maligned of all school subjects. Instead of wondering how best to communicate with a Hindu or a Buddhist or a Muslim (and how to assess *their* ability to communicate something of their faith in the relatively short time imposed by the medium of TV), I was faced with wondering how best *I* could communicate to an almost unanimously uninterested audience something of the world's various religions and why, in the first place, religion might be considered important enough to give it their attention. It is not an easy job and I have considerable respect for those teachers who do it well.

How has the sense of the value of religion been so thoroughly lost? If you doubt that it has, go into a classroom and watch how quickly the pupils turn off once the word 'religion', or anything suggestive of it, is mentioned. Their well-entrenched ignorance about and opposition to religious eduction (the dreadful 'it's just a waste of time/what use is it?' syndrome) would suggest that any indoctrination which schoolchildren are exposed to in this area comes more from those who are still fighting against what they (mistakenly) think this subject involves, rather than from those largely imagined—or remembered—foes who seek to use the classroom as an arena within which to convert others to their own religious outlook.

But what *does* religious education involve if it is not an attempt to convert to and instruct in a particular religion? That such a question is still so frequently asked would suggest the need for all those concerned with the subject to engage in a massive public relations exercise to exorcise once and for all the ghosts of the past. For of course the subject *is* haunted by memories of its old evangelical approach where preaching replaced teaching and the aim *was* very much to instil Christian virtues in every child. Here and there ghosts from the past remain, but by and large things have changed.

The answer to the question of what religious education ought to involve, which probably finds most favour in educational circles today, is something like this: pupils should be informed about religion from as neutral and objective a standpoint as possible, one which does not attempt to exert undue influence over what, at the end of the day, they choose to believe or disbelieve. In other words, they ought to be taken on a guided tour of the hall of mirrors and left to reach their own conclusions about what they see there.

I would not for a minute advocate a return to the singular, evangelical approach which has done so much to rob the subject of any respectable educational credentials (and has probably alienated many potential believers from all but the most immature brand of Christian Faith). However, preferable though the hall of mirrors style of religious education may be, it often gives insufficient attention to the question of the value of religion (something which the old approach was simply able to assume). Given the widespread loss of any real sense of religion's value, it would seem imperative to preface any tour of the hall of mirrors with a clear account of why it is being undertaken. In addition to a *knowledge about* religions, some sense of the *value of* religion ought surely to be fostered, for without it, no matter how many fascinating and colourful reflections we explore (and there is no shortage of these), the whole exercise will, in the end, strike those undertaking it as a rather pointless trudge around a series of meaningless names, ideas and images.

To suggest to children in a religious education class that religion has its own special value and is something worthy of their serious consideration, is no more to lapse into preaching or indoctrination than it would be for a music teacher to argue for the value of music (this is quite different from insisting that Beethoven is best). And just as musicians don't study bad music, even though there is plenty of it about, there is no reason why religious education teachers should be apologetic about concentrating on religion at its best. The problem remains, though, of how to communicate effectively in the context of the classroom the fact that the study of religion is a worthwhile project.

How is it possible to convey to a child something of the immensely humanizing and civilizing potential of true religion (whether this is Christian, Hindu, Jewish, Muslim, Buddhist or Sikh in orientation)? How can it be shown how important it is to go in at doorways we have labelled 'foreign', 'them', 'stupid', and really examine what is there? How can we explain the perilous proximity of the most barbarous savagery to the 'harmless' writing of racist and religious slogans on jotter covers (a depressingly common habit)? Such questions recur persistently and chase around the mind like Zen Buddhist *koans*. If we cannot find effective answers to them, our failure will have added in no small way to the likelihood that the hall of mirrors will ring with the sound of breaking glass, rather than offering a fascinating opportunity to look at ourselves and the world we live in from all sorts of new angles. Properly approached, it offers a veritable spiritual kaleidoscope whose potential for insight has scarcely been tapped. Even if we receive bruises going in at every religious doorway, and feel no compelling reason to remain when once inside, the exercise itself is still important. We cannot afford to ignore it if we aspire to be religiously educated.

Notes

1   'Hall of Mirrors' was a 10 programme series made by Scottish Television for national transmission on Channel Four. It was broadcast over the period 10 January 1985–7 March 1985.

11

Same House, Different Worlds

In 1885, Max Müller—who is often dubbed 'the father of comparative religion'—remarked to one of his house guests who did not
believe that they had been created by a loving deity:

> If you say that all is not made by design, by love, then you may be in
> the same house, but you are not in the same world with me.[1]

In the century since then, British society has become increasingly
pluralistic, such that, adopting Müller's terminology, although
Christian, Muslim, Sikh, Jew, Hindu and unbeliever may all be
cheek by jowl in the same overcrowded house, they seem to
occupy and look out on very different worlds indeed. For education—and particularly for religious education—the question that
is increasingly posed by such diversity is this: should we divide the
house of society into separate units so that those who believe that
the world is Christian may be educated accordingly, whilst those
who are Muslim may be taught in an Islamic context, Jews schooled
in a Jewish setting and so on, or should we try to educate people of
different faiths together? Should we, in other words, countenance
the fracturing of society along the seams already marked out by
the differing religious convictions of its various groups, in order
that they can set up their own schools and educate their children
in an atmosphere congenial to their *particular* faith, or should we
try to foster a common programme of education for all, which
acknowledges and addresses a situation of *many* faiths?

In trying to answer a question of such basic importance one
might expect some guidance to issue from the ideals enshrined in
the United Nations Universal Declaration of Human Rights. And
indeed at first sight this document *would* appear to provide grounds
for favouring *integrated* rather than separate schooling, for it states
that:

> Education shall be directed to the full development of the human
> personality and to the strengthening of respect for human rights and

fundamental freedoms. It shall promote understanding, tolerance and friendship among all national, racial or religious groups.[2]

Since such understanding and tolerance between members of the different groups in society could presumably best be fostered if they were discouraged from building educational walls around their ethnic and religious identities, but were, instead, schooled together in an open and non-divisive fashion, the matter might seem well on the way to being settled. Such a straightforward reading of Article 26 is, alas, impossible. Apart from anything else, it goes on to state that:

> Parents have a prior right to choose the kind of education that shall be given to their children.[3]

And, not unreasonably, many parents want to see their children educated according to the principles laid down by their own religion. For many, this means opting for separatist schooling at an establishment which is explicitly Christian, Muslim or whatever in its approach. Even though a parent's choice might (unintentionally) act to frustrate some of the ideals sought by the Declaration of Human Rights—ideals, we must remember, whose realization is vital for peaceful co-existence in a world of differences—that choice is still upheld as sacrosanct. If we want to argue against religious separatism in education, as I do here, then unless we wish to deny this prior right of parental choice (which I do not) we can only try to alert parents to the massive responsibility of their decision and explain that separate schooling—especially on matters relating to religion—risks baring and reinforcing those deadly divisions which run just beneath the surface of our precarious corporate existence.

Of course separate schooling according to religious division is already a well-established feature of the educational life of this country, with a basic divide running between Catholic and non-Catholic schools. Moreover, still in the public domain, the churches—especially the Church of England—have a significant influence both at school and at college level, whilst in the private sector various denominational groups often exercise a controlling interest. In a sense, these divisions have become so much a part of our educational system that the question of whether or not it is, in fact, a good thing to divide schooling in this way tends not to be seen as a particularly live issue. Whether or not it breeds contempt, familiarity leads to a lamentably uncritical acceptance of what we are used to.

Such a *laissez-faire* acceptance will surely be forced to re-examine the issue of separate schooling on religious grounds in the face of the emergence of a powerful new factor in the debate, namely the growing pressure from Britain's substantial Muslim community to set up their own schools. There are already independent Muslim schools operating in Britain. Representatives of the country's two million Muslims are keen that the number of such schools should be increased and that they should qualify for voluntary-aided status. After all, if public funds continue to be given to the Church of England, Roman Catholics and Jews for the purpose of maintaining *their* educational establishments, why should Islamic schools not also qualify for such finance?

The grounds on which the Swann Committee felt unable to recommend the setting up of separate denominational schools are instructive,[4] for they clearly recognize the extent of Muslim feeling on this subject. Their decision not to make such a recommendation was based precisely on the fear that it might lead to a sudden flood of Muslim schools which, so they reckoned, would simply encourage potentially anti-social religious and racial divisions. Such a fear has motivated decisions before Swann's. Thus Bradford Metropolitan Council resisted the campaign of its Asian Parents' Association to turn 5 local comprehensives into voluntary-aided establishments, on the grounds that such schools would establish a ghetto environment which would further polarize Muslim and non-Muslim. Instead, Bradford opted for their by now well-known 'celebration of diversity' and introduced a pioneering policy of multicultural education into all schools in the region. Similarly, in a response to the Swann Report (recorded in their discussion paper on religious education in a multi-faith society) the National Union of Teachers stated its view that the setting up of separate Muslim schools would be unhelpfully divisive and would simply militate against the integration of Muslims into society at large.

Unless we are to accept the highly dubious premise that *well-established* divisions are acceptable in a way that new ones are not, then the fears which troubled the Swann Committee, Bradford Council, the NUT and many others who view moves towards separate Muslim schools with alarm, must surely apply to any sort of religious separatism—indeed to any sort of educational separatism at all which sets up harmfully divisive walls in the classroom (whether these are built on differences of wealth, race or religion). Discriminating between old and new divisions seems merely to grant the former type the status of that most questionable of creatures in the intellectual bestiary, the sleeping dog who is allowed to lie, although there is, of course, one important distinction between old and new aspects of the debate on religious separatism, namely the fact that any line tracing out a contour of separate Islamic schooling would tend to mark out and emphasize not only religious but also *racial* differences. This important distinction notwithstanding, any examination of the pros and cons of having Muslim schools must surely raise for review the whole question of the desirability of religious separatism—*in whatever form*—in education.

The nature of religious education in state schools is often cited as an important factor in arguments advanced for separate Muslim schools. Religious education, it is claimed, is indoctrinatory rather than educational, it is Christian dominated and biased in its presentation. Moreover, the curriculum affords little place to the study of religion, and this whole subject area, already devalued in pupils' eyes by the negligible amount of time allotted to it, is rendered even less significant by the fact that it is often taught by non-specialists with few resources. As such, religious education seems to display all the sorry characteristics of its least flattering cognomen—'the sick man of education'.[5] Understandably, those who consider a person's faith to be of paramount importance are worried lest the educational malaise, which they see infecting that very part of the curriculum which deals with religion, spreads over into their children's own religious outlook. On the other hand, if it is not simply Christian indoctrination or dangerously feeble and enfeebling, religious education is often supposed to encourage scepticism by adhering to the critical methodology of a Western scientific approach. Moreover, religious education tends to abstract religion from the whole fabric of life and to study bits of it in isolation, thus failing to see it as the importantly *integral* phenomenon which the adherents of many faiths believe it to be. Whilst such complaints about religious education are perhaps most commonly heard today from Muslim sources, they are also voiced by other religious groups. Indeed, the setting up of new evangelical Christian schools must surely be a cause for some concern since they often display the worrying phenomenon of separatism following the lines of fundamentalism, if not religious extremism.

Does the nature of religious education provide legitimate grounds for those who are committed to a particular faith (or who eschew religion altogether) to seek, on account of it, to school their children—whether about religion or in general—in some other setting? Let it be said straight away that religious education *is* sometimes so pitifully 'sick' in practice that such a reaction to it is perfectly understandable. The subject is often not taken particularly seriously (if it were, would so little time and money be devoted to it, and would there still be schools where the subject simply is not taught?) Moreover, even where it is taught, staff are not always properly qualified, nor are their intentions always in line with the aims laid down by those who make policy decisions about the subject (this was alarmingly illustrated in a recent survey of religious education teaching in Wales when a significant number of teachers responsible for the subject declared their task to be the spreading of the Christian faith).[6] Such worrying symptoms of educational sickness should, I suggest, be weeded out and cured rather than be used to try to legitimate a policy of separatism, for they simply do not characterize what religious education in its healthy state is trying to do.

It seems to me that underlying all those more sophisticated statements of aims which seek to direct it, modern religious education attempts two fundamental tasks, and it is hard to see how any genuine attempt to fulfil them could be taken as providing grounds for seeking religious separatism in a child's schooling. These aims are:

1   To educate pupils about the fact of religious diversity, *ie* to make them realize that different people believe different things. (This is not nearly so obvious as might be supposed—I have encountered otherwise quite well-informed classes who could not even *name* four different religions!)

2   To teach them the skill of seeing things from the other person's point of view. Such a skill demands respect and fosters tolerance. It does not require assent.

In neither of these endeavours, let it be noted, need the contentious issue of religious truth be raised.

Can there be any acceptable grounds—whether educational or religious—for wanting to exempt a child from such learning and to conduct his or her schooling about religion in a purely mono-faith way? Surely if we are ever to live peacefully together in the same house, whether of a single planet, a single nation, or a single city, we must acknowledge the basic fact of the different worlds of its citizens and learn how to understand, tolerate and respect their multi-various beliefs. Would a segregated system not seriously lessen our choice of doing this? A useful reminder of just how deadly the divisions which arise between 'us' and 'them' can be, and how such divisions can flourish in a mind which has *not* learned how to see things from the other person's point of view, comes in Hannah Arendt's compelling study of the banality of evil, *Eichmann in Jerusalem*. There she identifies as one of Eichmann's chief characteristics his apparent inability to stand in someone else's shoes and imagine what the world looked like from there.[7]

It cannot be repeated too often that religious education does not seek to make people religious, nor to foster scepticism within them. It seeks only to extend that most basic of all educational principles—the removal of ignorance—some little way into the religious realm. Of course it cannot *fully* inform those in its charge about the diverse riches of any great world faith. Those who criticize it for failing to do so misconstrue what is practicable within the realities imposed by time and resources. Inevitably, given the time and resources at its disposal, religious education can only skim the surface of such massive repositories of human learning and experience as Christianity, Islam, Hinduism, and so on. But if it shows something of the extent and variety of the sea of faith of which they form part, albeit at a surface level, and if it teaches an awareness of and respect for the depths beneath (depths which may be plumbed at home, church, mosque, temple, and so on), it will surely have performed a vital social task. Such a task would be rendered much more difficult in a setting where only one faith was represented among pupils and granted credence by the school. Is it asking too much of religious leaders (from all the different faiths) to acknowledge and endorse the importance of the two fundamental tasks of religious education?

I know of no world religion which does not somewhere in its moral code suggest as an important principle that we should respect other people. Yet history tells us that such codes have been deciphered again and again into the most barbaric acts of cruelty towards those of other faiths. Given the religiously plural nature of the world and our depressingly common tendency towards violent pseudo-religious tribalism, must we not try hard to discourage any outlook which may seek to educate children from within an exclusively singular, separatist religious stance, where other people's points of view may be ignored—or dismissed as mistaken or unimportant? Of course if religious education is to provide an effective means of offering education for all in this vitally important area of human experience, we must cure it of every last vestige of that sickness which still so often troubles it. This will require the co-operation of parents, teachers, politicians and representatives of the various religious groups. Such co-operation may, I hope, be encouraged by stressing the possible consequences of abandoning religious education to its illness and allowing religious separatism to take fresh root.

In 1830, James Doyle, Roman Catholic Bishop of Kildare, wrote:

> I do not see how any man, wishing well of the public peace, and who looks to Ireland as his country, can think the peace can ever be permanently established, or the prosperity of the country ever well secured, if children are separated, at the commencement of life, on account of their religious opinions. I do not know of any measures which would prepare the way for a better feeling in Ireland than uniting the children at an early age, and bringing them up in the same school, leading them to commune with one another and to form those little intimacies and friendships which often subsist through life.[8]

Alas, bitter enmity rather than friendship has often characterized relationships between the religious communities in Ireland. The sad story with its wealth of unhappy endings which is still unfolding in Ulster today surely provides an object lesson, more persuasive than any argument, as to why we should take pains to urge the case for religiously integrated schooling. One small but cheering sign of light in this area of considerable darkness—and perhaps a vindication of Bishop Doyle's analysis—is that integrated schools *are* now being set up in Northern Ireland with the precise aim of educating Protestant and Catholic children *together*. We can only hope that the savage stimulus required to bring such schools into being will not be needed on the British mainland before we realize the importance of Christian, Muslim, Jewish and Hindu children, together with children from all the other faiths which go to make up our plural society, communing together and forming 'those little intimacies and friendships' on which so much depends.

History, according to the cynic, is the story of how human beings never learn from their mistakes. In Northern Ireland, history has provided a vivid point of religious and educational reference right on our doorstep—can we not learn from it? At the end of the day, if we cannot, if we fail to learn how to live with and tolerate the different worlds of outlook co-existing in the only house we have, our religiously and politically plural planet, and if we allow that failure international expression, then it seems more than likely that extinction will be our ultimate reward. At a more local level, religiously integrated schooling surely edges us away from the smaller precipices of confrontation and violence which always exist in a plural society and which mirror on a manageable scale those massive rifts between nations which we often feel quite powerless to heal. Locally, globally, we are going to have to learn to live with each other's differences sooner or later, so why not make a small start in school?

Notes

1   Nirad Chaudhuri, *Scholar Extraordinary, The Life of Friedrich Max Müller*, London: 1974, p 345.
2   United Nations Universal Declaration of Human Rights, article 26.2.
3   Ibid., article 26.3.
4   *Education for All*, Report of the Committee of Inquiry into the Education of Children from Ethnic Minority Groups (The Swann Report), HMSO: 1985. See in particular chapter 8, 'Religion and the Role of the School: Religious Education and the "Separate" Schools Debate'.
5   Edwin Cox, 'Religious Education: the Matter of the Subject', in Christopher Macy (ed), *Let's Teach Them Right*, London: 1969, p 32.
6   See *Religious Education 11–18 in Wales*, Report of a Survey Conducted by the Welsh National Centre for Religious Education, Bangor: 1984.
7   Hannah Arendt, *Eichmann in Jerusalem, A Report on the Banality of Evil* (revised and enlarged edition), Harmondsworth: 1983, pp 47-8.
8   Quoted without source in literature from the Belfast Charitable Trust for Integrated Education.

12

The Skull on the Mantel

Lest the title of this chapter should gladden the hearts of those who see no place for religious education on the school curriculum and wish only for its speedy extinction, let me point out at once that the skull in question does not bear witness to its final demise, but stands rather as an arresting image of the vital choice which is presently before the subject's methodological consciousness. By vital choice I mean just that. One option offers religious education new life, but it stands between two others which are straightforwardly terminal and which would lead to situations where the head of the subject, severed from any respectable body of learning, could be mounted in the hall of history alongside all our other educational mistakes.

I have taken the image of a skull on the mantel from Thornton Wilder's description of a philosophers' club in Edinburgh. Whether Wilder's account (given in his novel *The Eighth Day*)[1] was purely fictional or not, I simply do not know. But the historicity of the image does not matter much in terms of its applicability to religious education. The club's members met for the purpose of discussing beliefs both past and present. Such discussions were, however, carried out with a strict objectivity, enforced by a prohibition on talking in the first or second person of the present tense. As a reminder of the rule, and as a punishment for those who infringed it, a skull stood grimly on the mantel and into it all offenders who spoke in terms of what 'I' or 'you' believe were required to place a fine.

Applying this image to religious education it is perhaps easiest, *first* of all, to see it as a bleak indictment of attempts to examine religion from a neutral standpoint. As the mood in the subject has changed from one favouring a singular and judgmental approach (*ie* where Christianity was the only religion considered and where that consideration presented it as true) to one favouring a pluralistic and non-judgmental approach (*ie* where there is an objective presentation of a range of religions without any *a priori* assumptions about truth, the critic might well point to the skull on the mantel as a death's head of neutrality which has presided over such a shift; a death's head whose baleful Medusa gaze, shorn of all expression of personal commitment, turns to stone each living faith it touches and sums up graphically the lifelessness which well-meaning impartiality can sometimes lead to.

Religion cannot be understood without belief, or so this interpretation of the image argues, and any attempt to do so does fatal violence to the subject matter. Rather than exploring live religion, this type of religious education ends up directing (or rather misdirecting) its attention, and that of those exposed to it, to a shell, a mere emptiness, a gruesome trophy of its own mistaken methodology. This interpretation of the skull on the mantel's bearing on religious education clearly identifies one dead end which the subject might find itself in, for there is no denying the dreadful dealing in dead fact which *can* result from a decision not to get involved.

The *second* way in which the image may be interpreted identifies another dead end. In it we find ourselves face to face not with the evidence of a methodological murder of the subject matter, but with the straightforward annihilation of reason. This version of the skull on the mantel sees it as symbolic of a retreat from thinking, where such minimal lip service is paid to our powers of reflection that they die—and the brain's place is taken by the husk of its erstwhile container. This second dead end runs parallel to the first (and 'run' is perhaps the operative word) for it is by fleeing blindly from the frightening prospect of a destructively neutral approach that this particular cul-de-sac is reached. Faced with the prospect of 'killing' religions by looking at them over-objectively, it is easy to abandon reason altogether in favour of faith and to reintroduce commitment as the only viable starting point from which to examine religion. And from being seen as the exclusively legitimate beginning to the whole process of religious education, it is not long before it is seen as its only legitimate end as well, such that some sort of replication of the teacher's commitment is attempted through the medium of the religious education class.

Here the skull on the mantel simply stands for the demise of reason, which in such versions of religious education is effectively detached from the whole process of becoming religiously educated. Doubtless under such conditions some headless body of belief might still manage to twitch out some automatic religious responses in empty imitation of a living, thinking being. But although some semblance of life may survive, this approach to the subject is as deadening as that of extreme and unimaginative neutrality. In one, it is religion which is stifled and smothered; in the other, it is the inquirer into religion.

If we run from the potentially deadening effect of neutrality back into the arms of a confessionalist approach, we are simply changing educationally valueless money from one bankrupt currency to another. Religious education must attempt to find a delicate balance between these two deadweights, either one of which would inevitably lead to its extinction. On the one hand there is the deadweight of objectivity without humanity, neutrality taken to the extent of neutering. On the other hand there is the deadweight of subjectivity without critical reflection, commitment taken to the extent of compulsion. These are the horns of the dilemma faced by religious education. Is there some middle way between them? Many observers think not.

I believe that the solution lies in a *third* possible interpretation of the skull on the mantel, an interpretation which refuses to take fright at the undoubtedly intimidating aspects which both neutrality and commitment possess, which refuses to be startled into the simplistic decision to choose *either* objectivity *or* subjectivity when faced with the perennially puzzling question of how to approach religion in the classroom. This *third* interpretation of the image of the skull on the mantel, which I would commend to all those who are charged with the task of ensuring religious education's continued survival, suggests that far from being some grisly reminder of decay—whether of faith or of reason—the skull is best seen as serving boldly constructive purposes.

Certain basic facts of anatomy redeem the skull from any purely funereal function which our first emotional reactions to it are likely to infer. For, quite apart from the more dramatic and imaginative aspects which have become associated with it, the skull is, quite simply, the necessary foundation for the face and the protection for the brain which gives sense to any expression which the face may make. I would suggest that the skull on the mantel provides a reminder that if we are to arrive at any proper understanding of a religion, we must remember that there is more to it than meets the eye, more to it than the superficiality of expression, but that to get beyond the level of the obvious—the face which every religion presents to the world—we must pass through much that may be frightening and unpleasant. Such a passage will not be easy, but it is surely preferable to attempt the journey than simply to advocate a policy of superficial mimicry or photographic descriptivism.

One dead end in religious education presents us with a body of doctrine severed from any reflective process and says 'accept that'; the other presents us with a headful of details in isolation from anything which would make them come alive for us and says, 'this is religion'. Between them lies the subtler exercise of trying to understand what animates the numerous expressions that are met with on the multi-faceted face of human religiousness, what they mean to us and what—if anything—lies beyond them and gives them sense.

Given the nature of its subject matter, religious education must at times stress the objective side of its inquiry (what, precisely, does this particular text mean? when did such and such happen and how are such events best understood?) and at times the subjective side (what ought I to believe? what will happen when I die?). At all times it is—or ought to be—a *questioning* endeavour, and one in which the questioning is not done simply as a heuristic exercise in mental gymnastics, but because there is a deep-seated human need to ask such questions and to look for answers.

As Edward Hulmes has remarked, I think rightly, 'religious education is, *ultimately*, about choosing sides'.[2] I emphasize the 'ultimately' because before we can make any responsible decision about commitment, we need to stand back and seriously consider all the possibilities (and this includes the possibility of rejecting religion lock, stock and barrel). At all costs we must try to guard against premature belief blinding us to the truth, or a plethora of facts obscuring our need to answer certain questions.

Much that used to be considered religious education *has* died, the subject's critics will be pleased to learn (and its supporters even more so). Although religious education's lame and dead ducks have perhaps been more numerous, and have certainly received more public attention, than those in other areas of the curriculum, this ought not to blind us to the fact that *all* subjects have gone through reappraisals of what they are trying to achieve and how best to implement their aims via the constricting practicalities of the classroom. Such reappraisals should not be mistaken for death-throes. They are more frequently the birth-pangs of an emergent methodology.

What has emerged to symbolize religious education is not a series of skeletons in the educational cupboard whose rattling has done so much to discredit the subject and whose echoes still seem to bias many people's assessment of it, but a skull on the mantel, potent and paradoxical in the imagery it offers to characterize the subject's new identity. If religious education can only keep the balance between neutering neutrality and compulsory commitment (and I believe that under the right conditions it can) then there would seem to be a reasonable hope that there might be encouraged an attitude of mind which could finally look, if not with equanimity or understanding, then at least with some degree of intelligent informedness and well-practised inquiry at the skull *inside*, the reminder of our precarious and mysterious mortality, about which the whole business of religion is, in the end, so much concerned.

Perhaps the many interpretative straws which I have loaded upon it here will only only serve to break the back of my chosen analogy, rather than to suggest three ways in which it can portray—albeit obliquely—the directions which religious education must choose between. If, like the proverbial camel, I *have* done it to death, then I can only hope that my readers will have been brought down somewhere along the way with a strong enough jolt to shatter any misconceptions which they might have had concerning this most maligned of subjects and to awaken them to the enormous potential worth of religious education.[3]

Notes

1   Thornton Wilder, *The Eighth Day*, London: 1967, p 167.
2   Edward Hulmes, *Commitment and Neutrality in Religious Education*, London: 1979, p. 103. My emphasis.
3   The image of the skull on the mantel is further explored in Chapter 6 of my *In the Hall of Mirrors, Some Problems of Commitment in a Religiously Plural World*, London: 1986, pp 108-27.

13

The Twelfth Window

In one of the Grimm brothers' fairy tales we read of a princess in whose bedroom there were twelve windows looking out in all directions. Out of the first window she could see more clearly than anyone in the kingdom, out of the second even better, and so on to the twelfth, through which, so we are told, 'she could see everything on the earth or beneath it'.[1] The princess refused to marry anyone who could not manage to hide himself from her scrutiny. Nearly a hundred prospective suitors had attempted to elude her gaze, but all had failed long before she had had to look beyond the fourth or fifth magic window in her room. These unfortunates were promptly beheaded for their pains. At last, the hero of the story attempts to win her hand. Passing successfully though a number of ordeals, he manages to find someplace to hide where, even assisted by the twelfth window, the royal eye is unable to see. Angry that she has finally been beaten, the princess smashes this all-seeing pane, at which point the hero emerges from his hiding place and claims her as his bride.

Television sometimes seems to act rather like the twelfth window in this story. It shows a vast range of things which are happening, or have happened, on, beneath and above the earth. Few events seem able to hide from its powerful scrutiny. Of course, to a large extent—unlike the princess's window— the wide-angled vision afforded by TV is something to be welcomed. For instead of resulting merely in the gratuitous beheading of innocents, it does much to put to the sword ignorance, loneliness, boredom and other such unwanted experiences. It would be foolish indeed to underestimate the *positive* potential of TV in human affairs.

But it would be even more foolish to suppose that it invariably acts in this way, as some sort of benign lens which always enables us to see further and more clearly. Unlike the windows in the story, which provide successively penetrating panes through which to look, the operation of television is more accurately presented if we see it as offering a series of windows where we can be taken *either* in the direction of more acute vision, *or* towards an increasingly impaired outlook. Whilst accepting that, at its best, TV provides a twelfth window of enormous value—educational, religious and otherwise—it is on one of its less positive aspects, one of its sight-impairing windows (which I suspect are more common) that I wish to concentrate here. For the bulk of TV, I will argue, looks out from a spiritual wilderness and presents this as a true picture of how things are. As such, it constitutes a formidable barrier to effective religious education.

Standing in the great rain forest of South America long before television had even been dreamed of, Charles Darwin once remarked that:

> No one can stand in these solitudes unmoved, and not feel there is more in man than the mere breath of his body.[2]

It is precisely such a feeling of transcendence, a sense that there is more to human life than the everyday, which animates the teachings of the great world faiths. Whether that transcendent something is best thought of on a personal scale as Soul, Spirit, Self, Atman, or Selflessness; or, on a universal scale, as God, Brahman, Nirvana, the Tao, an impersonal Absolute or a chilling Emptiness, is not, I would argue, the business of religious education, at least at school level, where it must instead concentrate its efforts on two prior tasks. Making sure *first*, that pupils recognize the existence of a spiritual dimension in human experience (a dimension which can be referred to in shorthand by Darwin's 'There is more to man than the mere breath of his body'); and, *second*, that they are given some information about, and provided with some skill in approaching, various modes of spiritual thinking. Described as such, the task of religious education might not sound too difficult, or at least no more difficult than that of any other subject. Alas, whereas in the great rain forests of South America Darwin's insight might not need much in the way of teaching to dawn on the majority of human minds, in the modern urban jungles in which so much of our learning occurs, such a basic sensitivity to life's spiritual dimension can by no means be taken for granted.

Part of the reason for the blunting of our spiritual sensitivity which seems to have taken place in modern times may have to do with the way in which our society, often at least partially because of TV, has lost touch with some of the elemental facts of life and the fundamental religious questions which they raise. The 'Primal Curriculum' (see pp 34-40) has been obscured and forgotten. For example, the sociologist Peter Berger has observed that 'modern society has banished the night from consciousness so far as this is possible',[3] whereas John Hick notes that the average American child, before he reaches the age of fourteen, will have witnessed some 18,000 deaths presented via the artificial daylight of television.[4] If we contrive to 'forget' about the realities of mortality and death, is it any wonder that our basic religious sensibility (what I am simply terming our spirituality) may suffer?

Whatever the reasons for our apparent 'transcendence blindness' may be, one of the healthiest plants in our familiar jungle (and, according to some, one of the most addictive and poisonous) is undoubtedly television. We are born, live and die in the light which its flickering pictures provide. Its spread has been positively prodigious. Like some super-resilient creeper, its tendrils have curled around every available surface area. Our visual harvesting of the diverse fruits it bears occupies a considerable portion of waking hours. It has seeded itself deeply in our experience and provides the basic educational milieu from which millions draw the bulk of the informational raw material on which their opinions, interests and beliefs are founded. Its programmes pollinate our minds with values which are far removed from Darwin's assessment of human nature, which allowed for something more than meets the eye, something more than can be pictured on the screen.

Let me emphasize that I am *not* talking either about those programmes which might themselves be termed 'religious' ('This is the Day', 'Songs of Praise', 'Highway' *etc*, nor about those programmes which, whilst not in any way devotional or evangelistic, take religion as their subject matter. The first group, which often falls within the general title of 'religious broadcasting', is of very little educational use and cannot always be exempted from the charge of contributing to television's generally negative spiritual/religious influence. The second group (programmes like the 'Believe it or Not' series, made specifically for schools; or the BBC's phenomenally successful 'The Long Search', first broadcast in 1977 and long due a re-run) can be of enormous educational worth and are sometimes quite exemplary in content and presentation—but they constitute a minute proportion of television output, can only claim minority viewing and are likely to be seen very much in (and judged through) the light of more popular programmes. It is television in general, the ordinary daily dose of programming, rather than some of its specialist output, that I am most concerned with here. In particular, my concern is with the fact that TV seems to act as a profoundly negative force in terms of our apprehension and appreciation of life's spiritual or religious dimension.

Malcolm Muggeridge once suggested that, 'it is a terrible fact that the average citizen spends some eight years of his life looking into a television screen'.[5] Whether or not they are 'terrible' is hard to say, but when we look at some of the basic facts about human consumption of TV, they are certainly apt to be rather startling. For instance:

> Television is now the foremost leisure activity in most families. On a typical day 38 million people (in the UK) tune in and watch, on average, for two or three hours.[6]

> The average child in the United States has watched between 10,000 and 15,000 hours of television by the time he is sixteen years old, and by the time he reaches eighteen he will have watched more hours of television commercials than an undergraduate spends in class during his four year university course. Similar figures probably could be cited for most other countries where television is highly developed.[7]

> The average man spends more time watching TV than any other activity except his work and sleeping.[8]

> In 1955 over a third of UK households had TV sets; by 1960, 8 out of 10 households had a set; and by the mid 1970s 9 out of 10 had one set with an increasing number having more than one.[9]

Indeed, given some of these observations (which, incidentally, make no mention of video, a further and often disturbing feature of our television environment,[10] we might feel that the London Borough of Enfield's recent advertisement for primary teachers is not quite accurate. The advertisement in question (published in various papers—see, for example, page 46 of the *Times Educational Supplement* on 12 June, 1987) shows a child's drawing of Mum, Dad and teacher, three matchstick figures, the leading lights in a kindergarten *dramatis personae*, above which is the caption: 'After Mums and Dads, probably the most influential figure in a young person's life'. But might we not argue that TV, rather than teacher, should feature as the third formative force in the child's world? As one commentator has put it:

> After parents and before school, *television* is the primary educator of our children. It has become a dominant voice in our lives and a major agent of socialization in the lives of our children.[11]

But even though it may claim so large a part of our attention, why should television, that homely familiar which sits in the corner of all our lives, a never-ending source of entertainment, instruction, and diversion, be cast in the role of spiritual villain, helping to hide from ourselves an awareness of something of value beyond the mundane world of breath and blood? Such an accusation rests on two important assumption: that whilst, by and large, TV endorses and promulgates the materialistic values of society, religion seeks to challenge them and offer an alternative outlook.

Of course it can be argued that, far from being anti-religious or non-spiritual, TV now effectively *fulfils* many of the functions which would have been performed by religion in times past. But although there are indeed many close parallels between them, we surely have to ask if this supposed fulfilment of religious functions by TV is not just *apparent* fulfilment by an artificial substitute, a pseudo-religion, which cannot adequately replace the real thing. Analysing the situation in Australia, Peter Horsfield suggests that 'television needs to be seriously considered as an operative religious faith for a large proportion of the population'.[12] He continues:

> That television is effective in creating common belief patterns is demonstrated by research. Studies show consistently that heavy viewers of television begin to reflect the perceptions and myths which television subtly propagates. They also suggest that the messages of television bypass critical mental faculties and are absorbed impressionistically within the subconscious. The challenge which this massive alternative belief system, which is being worshipped for 4½ months of 12 hour days each year by most Australians, poses for traditional religious faith, has yet to be taken seriously by scholars and educators.[13]

Similarly, Gregor Goethals argues that TV has largely taken over from traditional religious symbols and icons the task of satisfying one of our deepest longings—to feel part of a community. On the grand scale, we only need to think of the ways in which TV renders some form of sharing or participation possible in great national events—a royal wedding, a state funeral, a memorial service, a papal visit—to see how it acts in this way; and on a more everyday basis, millions share the fortune of 'soap opera' characters, and 'participate' in the adventures of serial stories and screen dramas. It is largely through TV that many images of social integration now make their way into the psyche of modern nations, asserting and reinforcing the elements of a common culture. As Goethals puts it,

> much of what people think about the 'good life', the roles of men and women, technology, or the changing patterns of family and political life, emerges from the television set.[14]

The trouble is, the TV version of the 'good life' is one in which spirituality seems to play very little part. Would the average viewer, feasting on a diet of 'Dallas' and 'Dynasty', 'EastEnders' and 'The Price is Right', 'The A-Team' and 'Dempsey and Makepeace', together with whatever advertisements and news bulletins occur in their interstices, be encouraged to think that 'there is more in man than the mere breath of his body'? Such programmes are set firmly in the here and now of immediately visible action and excitement, where the qualities and goals striven for and the values held up as praiseworthy and enviable tend to be somewhat superficial (wealth, physical beauty, violence, *etc*). As Jonathon Porritt puts it in *Seeing Green*, a book which, incidentally, provides numerous illustrations of the important relationship between environment and spirituality:

> As a teacher I knew only too well how much more powerful television is than school, churches, or even families in terms of creating a set of values or 'consensus' opinions. Day after day one is exposed to a totally distorted portrayal of people concentrating almost exclusively on the violent, the superficial, the selfish and the apathetic. At a time when we require the very best, we are fed a diet of the very worst. Television has become a tool of our mass-consumption society, reinforcing materialistic attitudes and wasteful habits.[15]

Of course it is still hotly disputed just what effect TV has on human behaviour. But at the very lowest assessment of damage, putting together some statistics into a single (albeit extreme) representative case, it is surely unlikely that a child who watches some 20 hours of TV every week, who may have witnessed around 18,000 screen deaths and over a quarter of a million advertisements by the time (s)he is 14 years old, and who will probably have viewed at least one 'video nasty', will be particularly well disposed either to the sort of ideals which education attempts to operate, or to the basic spiritual sensitivity without which religious education becomes a mere catalogue of dead facts. As Milton Shulman observed:

> In their complacency and equanimity, the British television public resembles smokers before there was any evidence that cigarettes could be responsible for cancer and heart disease.[16]

It is perhaps in advertising, although it is by no means confined to there, that the spiritually negative side of TV is most openly visible (see pp 29-33). Images replace ideas and reason is banished in a series of value-laden visual cameos where we are urged to view the ownership of non-essential products as virtually indispensable for some aspect of our supposed well-being. As one Christian critic has put it:

> the ideology inherent in advertising and the majority of programmes reveals the social sin and collective blindness condemned by Jesus.[17]

Such blindness fails to see that TV's consumerism encourages a small minority of the world's population 'to devour a huge amount of its resources whilst others drown in a sea of poverty'.[18] It hides from our sight a vision of our transient and mysterious mortality, the existential plight of creatures of an hour living precariously at the age of unnerving vastnesses of time and space.

If we are to understand the enormous difficulty facing religious education teaching today, and if we are to appreciate why TV tends to be such a spiritually negative force, it is, I think, important to stress just how disruptive religion is of many ordinary certainties and how critical it is of the values and models of identity thought to be adequate, or even admirable, by society at large (and which are repeatedly presented as such on television). To the extent that TV may be considered to mirror, amplify and reinforce conventional models of being, so it is likely to be unreceptive to the alternative models suggested by any religious vision which is rooted in the view that, 'there is more to man than the mere breath of his body'.

As Sallie McFague has stated with regard to the Christian tradition, 'every major reformation within the church has been sparked by the insight that the essence of Christianity does not support conventional standards'.[19] Similarly, in a fascinating essay entitled, 'A Devout Meditation in Memory of Adolf Eichmann', Thomas Merton has pointed out that the very concept of sanity as it is held to in modern society contains a fundamentally non-Christian element in its exclusion of love.[20] In other words, the Christian concept of identity, of who a person is and what (s)he should strive for, seems to challenge a central thread in the answers which Western society and its incessant television output give to questions of purpose and value. Far from belonging to society and endorsing its values unquestioningly, the Christian, according to Merton, should condemn as fundamentally misguided much of what is regarded as socially acceptable (even to the extent of questioning so basic a concept as sanity)—and, inevitably, such condemnation would encompass a great deal of television output. Harvey Cox puts the matter in a nutshell when he notes how the behaviour models put forward by the mass media 'often directly contradict the life goals Christianity celebrates'.[21]

After all, from the perspective of the eternal verities which all religions seek to move us towards, how can the values implicit in advertising, TV game shows, and most 'light entertainment' be seen as anything other than irredeemably and blindingly irrelevant? Yet it is just those values that are uppermost in the minds of many pupils. To break through them and instil an awareness of the radically different perspectives which are contained in religious outlooks, is an essential preliminary to any serious programme of religious education. But it is a preliminary that becomes increasingly difficult in a television culture, where the very notion that 'there might be more to man than the mere breath of his body', and that that element might constitute something of immense importance, is smothered by a veritable electronic avalanche of advice on how to avoid bad breath and keep the body beautiful, and thereby acquire some sort of dubious salvation that looks only to material possessions and poses for its attainment.

In teaching about transcendence, which is surely the basic task of religious education, we are addressing an audience whose mind-set has already been fundamentally affected by TV values. Unless we can make clear that some things can and do hide from the twelfth window of TV and that, at the end of the day, they may be more important than any of the pictures we watch and follow so avidly, then our spirituality, like the unfortunate suitors in the Grimm brothers' story, may face a beheading.

In *Thinkers of the East*, Idries Shah recounts the tale of the Sufi teacher who was asked by a curious pupil how he felt. The teacher replied, 'like one who has risen in the morning and does not know whether he will be dead by evening'. The pupil was puzzled to hear so apparently ordinary a reply coming from one who was famed for his wisdom. He complained rather disappointedly, 'But this is the situation of all men'. To which the teacher's retort was, 'Yes. But how many of them *feel* it?'[22] It seems to me that in view of the spiritual anaesthesia which TV tends to purvey, an important task of the modern religious educator must be to ensure that pupils come to realize for themselves (that they come to *feel*) some of the elemental existential facts which have always defined the human condition and which always will, no matter how thick a layer of sugar-coated trivia and effortless amusement our television environment may carelessly deposit on top of them. It is only when such facts are keenly felt that one can properly appreciate (and come to a responsible evaluation of) what the religious consciousness is driving at.

Writing long before television became so dominant a feature of our society, Henry David Thoreau once observed that 'moral reform is the effort to throw off sleep'.[23] This is surely a goal which morality, education and religion have in common—to wake us from the various slumbers of ignorance and distraction which so easily take our minds off the real world and the problems it poses, and substitute instead a scale of values and priorities which few people would really wish to live by if they stopped to think about it. Television has the potential to assist in the educative process of waking up (witness, for example, the impact of 'Live Aid'). As things stand at present, though, it seems more usually to act as a potent soporific.

Notes

1   The Brothers Grimm, *Fairy Tales* (with an introduction by Margaret W J Jeffrey), London: 1954, p 176. The story in which the image of the twelfth window occurs is 'The Seal'.
2   Quoted in Alan Moorehead, *Darwin and the Beagle*, Harmondsworth: 1973, p 86.
3   Peter L Berger, *A Rumour of Angels, Modern Society and the Rediscovery of the Supernatural*, Harmondsworth: 1971, p 95.
4   This statistic is a quoted by John Hick in *Death and Eternal Life*, London: 1976, p 86.
5   Malcolm Muggeridge, *Christ and the Media*, (the 1976 London Lectures in Contemporary Christianity), London: 1977, p 82.
6   Dave Morley and Brian Whitaker (eds), *The Press, Radio and Television, an Introduction to the Media*, London: n.d., p 21.
7   W E Biernatzki, *Catholic Communication Research, Topics and a Rationale*, London: 1978, p 9.
8   David Attenborough (former head of BBC2), quoted in Milton Shulman, *The Ravenous Eye, the Impact of the Fifth Factor*, London: 1973, p 1.
9   Morley & Whitaker (eds), op. cit., p 22.
10   For some of the more chilling aspects of video see Geoffrey Barlow & Alison Hill (eds), *Video Violence and Children*, London: 1985.
11   Jean Marie Hiesberger, 'The Ultimate Challenge to Religious Education', *Religious Education*, vol 76 (1981), p 357. My emphasis.
12   Peter Horsfield, 'Religious Dimensions of Television's Uses and Content', *Colloquium*, vol 17, no 2 (1985), p 62.
13   Ibid., p 66.
14   Gregor Goethals, *The TV Ritual, Worship at the Video Altar*, Boston: 1981, p 2.
15   Jonathon Porritt, *Seeing Green, the Politics of Ecology Explained*, Oxford: 1984, p 119.
16   Milton Shulman, op. cit., p 12.

17   Jeanne Cover, 'Theological Reflections: Social Effects of Television', *Religious Education*, vol 78 (1983), p 40.
18   Peg Slinger, 'Television Commercials: Mirror and Symbol of Societal Values', *Religious Education*, vol 78 (1983), p 35.
19   Sallie McFague, 'The Christian Paradigm', in Peter C Hodgson and Robert H King (eds), *Christian Theology, an Introduction to its Traditions and Tasks*, London: 1983, p 332.
20   Thomas Merton, *Raids on the Unspeakable*, London: 1977, pp 31–2.
21   Harvey Cox, *The Seduction of the Spirit*, New York: 1973, p 15.
22   Idries Shah, *Thinkers of the East, Studies in Experientialism*, London: 1971, p 122.
23   Henry David Thoreau, *Walden, or Life in the Woods*, London: 1912, p 78.

14

Taming the Tiger

At a recent conference of Caribbean churches called to examine the
way in which the influx of American TV programmes was affecting
the area's indigenous culture, a delegate remarked that those who
are worried about TV often behave like a man with a tiger outside
his door who imagines that the tiger is the only problem. He forgets
that the problem is not so much the beast itself as *what he is going
to do about it.*[1]

The image is, I think, an appealing one, and one which is not
restricted in relevance to the Caribbean alone. For not only does it
identify the sort of shirking of responsibility which is commonplace
when we turn our attention to television (how often, after all, do we
hear calls for the TV *audience*, rather than the programme makers,
to act in a responsible manner?), but a tiger is also a rather apt
symbol for some aspects of the mass media, and of television in
particular. Colourful, exciting, fast-moving and violent, our taste
in programming surely has some definite feline affinities.

The Caribbean churchman's analogy invites one important
revision for home use. Given the prevalence of the mass media
in contemporary British society, it is surely not so much a case
of there being a tiger stalking about *outside* our door, as of its
being in the same room with us. Indeed if the Scottish Film Council's recently published *Media Education: Curriculum Guidelines*
are correct in their assessment, the average pupil is quite accustomed to sharing his living space with a veritable crowd of media
tigers:

> This week and every week Scottish schoolchildren will spend an aver-
> age of twenty four and a half hours watching television, nearly six
> hours listening to radio and music, and three hours reading comics,
> newspapers, magazines and books.[2]

Such a high rate of media consumption, I would suggest,
ought vividly to underline the importance of fostering adequate
communication skills.

Unfortunately, 'communication skills' is one of the vaguest labels in the educational glossary. It can be attached to almost anything from basic literacy to video production and tends to occupy an uncertain multidisciplinary territory on the school curriculum which, when you actually set out to find it, sometimes leads to the suspicion that, in terms of the conventions of pedagogical map-reading, 'multidisciplinary' means little more than 'non-existent'. Of course it occurs in more explicit form in tertiary education, but even there its frequent pairing with media studies, English, drama, general studies and so on makes one uneasy about its status as an independent subject. Part of the problem is doubtless the sheer implicatedness of communication in almost everything we do, for it is, quite simply, a fundamental part of being human. As the German theologian Wolfgang Bartholomäus put it, 'one cannot *not* communicate'.[3] As such, it might be argued that 'communication skills' are taken in *en passant*; they are so integral to *any* learning progress that there is no need to abstract them for special consideration. They are automatically acquired—unless there is some particular *problem*, in which case 'communication skills' can become another euphemism for remedial teaching.

Clearly, various communication skills are indeed fostered in all sorts of important ways throughout the curriculum. My concern is that implicit learning may not give enough attention to the question of personal communicative responsibility. It is one thing to understand how to create an effective advertisement or radio script, produce an eye-catching poster, write a letter, essay, screenplay or job application, quite something else to realise just how essential the individual's integrity is in the performance of each of these communicative acts. Whilst it is important to ensure that pupils understand that, for example, television news is not the straightforward window in the world which many of its viewers assume it to be, the significance of such a lesson would surely be increased if, alongside a recognition of the various factors which render news a less than objective exercise, a sensitivity was cultivated to the way in which many of our own day-to-day utterances are laden with all sorts of values which we may not consciously intend. Codes of conduct for fair reporting, or for advertising which is 'legal, decent, honest and truthful', are surely doomed to failure unless they are undergirded by a personal sense of fair play in each individual's approach to his or her own communicative activities.

The re-visioning of communication skills which I am suggesting would be one in which practical, critical and moral considerations would be given equal weight. Whilst the practical and critical aspects of communication may be dealt with adequately already, whether in English, drama, or media education, there seems to be a definite need for more attention to be given to the morality of this fundamental human activity and for the inter-relationships which exist between its practical, critical and moral aspects to be highlighted. Might religious education not provide a suitable ready-made forum in which some of the issues which arise here could be discussed?

Since we are probably all familiar with those who, on religious grounds, raise cries of protest about violence, sex and bad language on the small screen, it is important to stress that this suggestion of a possible role for religious education in a re-visioned programme of communication skills does not come from the same stable of thought, or indeed even from one closely adjoining it. Such protests (to continue our analogy) seem to see the media tiger as a sensual marauder of our most cherished values. The question of the individual as a communicator charged with responsibility in sending and receiving messages is scarcely looked at, as TV is cast in the role of monster whose bestial appetites can be blamed for all sorts of social ills and whose alleged depravities can easily be presented as constituting a particular threat to the young.

Obviously, the content of particular programmes may sometimes be a matter for concern (or, more commonly, the content of particular video productions—the findings of the recent Parliamentary Group Video Enquiry into video violence and children, for example, contain some truly chilling educational implications), but criticisms which never leave a sex and violence orbit seem to me to miss the point. In his seminal work, *Understanding Media*, Marshall McLuhan one remarked that the content of any medium is like 'the juicy piece of meat carried by the burglar to distract the watchdog of the mind'.[4] Too often, those who comment on TV from a religious standpoint have wasted their time worrying at gobbets of tempting flesh while, beyond their outrage at mere explicitness, a rather more serious crime is being perpetrated. In urging that religious education pay some attention to the morality of communication, to questions of value, responsibility and truth as they pertain to the media, the content of particular programmes would be a matter of only very secondary relevance.

In his excellent study, *Television and Religion*, in which he argues convincingly that TV is usurping many of the traditional functions of the church, William Fore stresses the importance of media education. In America, he observes, it:

. . . is just beginning to take hold in the public schools, and is almost altogether missing in the churches. Yet teaching people to understand what the media are doing to them . . . could scarcely be more important to educators and church leaders.[5]

It would be a pity, in this country, if church and school did not exert themselves to make sure that television is not the final victor in the battle for our souls which Fore assures us is being waged. Such exertion, I would suggest, might usefully take the form of producing teaching material (for use in the religious education class) which focussed on the whole question of media, communication and values. The mythology and consequences of advertising (already an area of concern for some theologians) might be the most obvious place to begin.

Such material is not without encouraging precedent. Despite Fore's rather pessimistic assessment, there has, in fact, been some first-rate educational work produced by various religious groups in America over the last few years. Perhaps most notable have been the efforts of the Media Action Research Centre in producing a comprehensive programme which, incidentally, has just been introduced in Britain through a project being run by the Mothers' Union).[6] The Episcopal Ad project has taken religious thinking on advertising to a new level of sophistication and it is notable that the highly acclaimed journal *Media and Values*,[7] which is of considerable educational interest, is produced by an ecumenical Christian group. That some sort of co-operative alliance between religious education and media education is far from being an unrealistic idea, gains further credence from certain developments on this side of the Atlantic too. Some of the publications already sponsored by the Jesuit-run Centre for the Study of Communication and Culture in London,[8] and some of the educational activities of the World Association for Christian Communication (WACC) are particularly important. *Media Development*, the quarterly journal published by WACC, forms a valuable resource for teachers of religious education and media education alike.[9]

It is perhaps in the mass media which surround us, and particularly in television, rather than in face to face interpersonal communication, that the extent of the inadequacy of mere skilfulness becomes evident. In advertising, for example, few people would deny that highly effective communication skills are being employed. But are the values implicit in the majority of consumer ads really the sort of thing that we want to see in our society? The mechanics of advertising may be flawlessly efficient, but what of its morality? Soap operas (like *EastEnders*) and adventure serials (like *The A-Team*) may be effectively entertaining (may, indeed, qualify for the ultimate accolade of being 'good television'), but what sort of values are they inculcating and reinforcing in those who watch? The techniques which are employed in their production may be professionally brilliant, but what of the theology they carry with them? Are they the sorts of communicative models we want to put before our children?

Robert Fisk, Middle East correspondent for *The Times* and winner of the 1987 Valiant for Truth Media Award (presented annually by the London-based Order of Christian Unity), has pointed out the way in which media clichés give us a distorted view of things. As a small example he cites the way in which, in the Western press, Syria is almost invariably tagged 'Soviet backed' and Kalashnikov 'Russian made', whilst Israel and M-16 are rarely if ever accompanied by 'American backed' or 'American made'.[10] If we are to avoid the potentially misleading pictures which may thus be engendered, we must teach pupils to be acute, careful and accurate communicators. Their skill must extend beyond an acquired expertise in using what Fisk rightly terms the 'dead language'[11] of cliché, whose vocabulary serves only to render things into simplistic (and often dangerous) caricatures and to blur the understanding.

It needs only a brief glimpse at the extremes which irresponsible communication leads to, to see the importance of fostering a skilled sense of responsibility in this area. For instance, the excellent 'Anne Frank in the World' exhibition, which visited many British galleries in 1987, made mention of many examples of contemporary right-wing books and news-sheets which deny that the holocaust ever happened. The destruction of the European Jews by the Nazis, so such publications seek to assure us, is no more than a fantastic Zionist party story planted to discredit National Socialism. That media can be used to present an alternative, and false, reality, to rewrite history so it accords with the author's politics is, alas, not something that is confined to the pages of Orwell's *Nineteen Eighty-Four*. Re-visioned communication skills seem to me to be an important way of making sure that the pictures of the world thus presented are not allowed to multiply and take hold.

Given the ease with which supposedly documentary material can now be convincingly fabricated, fostering such communication skills ought surely to be seen as an urgent educational priority. In a world where for example, the computerized digital retouching of photographs can make it appear as if almost anything has really happened, it is important not only that pupils know something of the power of the image to convince, and that they are made aware of the existence of sophisticated image-altering techniques, but that they also understand those theological and moral arguments which would curb the use of such techniques.

Whilst it is useful up to a point, I would suggest that the analogy of the tiger suggested by the Caribbean churchman is, in the end, misleading, for it risks exteriorizing the whole problem and failing to perceive the fact that the tiger is best seen not as something which stalks around outside our homes, or even within them, but that, ultimately, it is something which lies inside each one of us. It is only when we fail to tame our own tigers of communication that they are likely to grow up into media monsters. After all, every advertisement, every film, every piece of propaganda or truthful reporting, every constitutive image and utterance in the multi-faceted media which surround us, has its genesis in an individual human author. That such individual genesis can, through modern communications technology, be magnified and disseminated so that an audience numbered in millions may be addressed, means that special care needs to be taken to ensure that the individual is educated in such a way as to be able to shoot down any man-eaters that may have escaped from someone else's communicative bestiary (publications which deny the holocaust are an extreme case in point, but there are less serious examples every day in the press and on TV), and to ensure that his own communications approximate to rather more worthy ideals. It is worth remembering that there is a very real sense in which careless talk can cost lives.

The re-visioning of communication skills which I would like to see, would seek to emphasize and explore the responsibility which each one of us has as members of that most powerful of communications organizations, not CBS, NBC, the BBC or News International, but the human race. People, after all, are the most fundamental (although curiously neglected) of the mass media. 'Taming the Tiger' would not involve seeing the media as some sort of non-human third party which has somehow managed to implicate itself into our lives and run amok in the fastnesses of our corporate existence. Instead, it would involve educating and developing the tiger of communication which dwells in every individual (and is reflected in the mass media). In this endeavour religious education and media education may have an important joint role to play. Both need to provide the pupil with a firm grounding in what we might call 'image education'. There is, I believe, a particularly pressing need for attention to be given to this area within religious education in the present British media context.

Writing in *The Seduction of the Spirit*, the American theologian Harvey Cox confessed to feeling uneasy about the fact that most of those responsible for religious education in the States 'live and work on tiny rafts of written pages adrift in an ocean of images.[12] Much the same imbalance exists in Britain. By and large the training of religious education specialists takes place via the print-based disciplines of theology and religious studies. Professional qualifications, too, tend to be typographic rather than pictorial in emphasis, despite some attention given to 'audio-visual skills'. And yet it is via *images*, not words, that most pupils will now most frequently encounter religion—and many other aspects of life as well. We are living at a time when the image seems to be in the ascendant and philosophers are talking about 'the retreat from' (George Steiner) and the 'humiliation of' (Jacques Ellul) the word.[13] Despite this, words still continue to dominate the educational process.

The extent to which TV can be thought to inform and educate as well as entertain is, of course, uncertain. Nor is it clear what relationship exists between the print-based teaching which occurs at school and the images which fall on our minds in such profusion from the small screen. How is classroom teaching about Islam, for example, affected by the vivid images of Iranian anger which have been flashed from our screens in the wake of the Salman Rushdie affair? Can a classroom grounding in Muslim beliefs avoid being eclipsed by pictures of book-burning in Bradford or marches in Edinburgh? How can the study of Christianity address the mind which has been fed almost daily images of sectarian violence in Northern Ireland? Can education provide deeper and more serious meanings for 'Protestant' and 'Catholic' than those which are likely to be absorbed from news reports of happenings in Ulster? In what ways do the many images of inter-religious conflict from around the world (in India between Hindu and Sikh, in the Middle East between Jew and Muslim, in Tibet between Buddhism and Chinese communism) affect our teaching about these faiths?

It is surely an area for urgent educational research to try to tease out some of the consequences of trying to educate in the shadow of insistent and prolific TV images (which are, of course, further reinforced by magazines, advertising and the press). Writing in 1964, Marshall McLuhan observed that 'the educational establishment, founded on print, does not yet admit any other responsibilities'.[14] Two decades later, such an admission still seems slow in coming. Despite the pre-eminence of the image in our culture, education remains loath to look up from the printed page and give it the attention it deserves. It is worth remembering

McLuhan's grim prediction, which we mentioned earlier, that education might become little more than 'civil defence against media fallout'.[15] Such fallout now seems to be accumulating at an alarming rate in many areas of the curriculum.

In *Amusing Ourselves to Death*, educationalist Neil Postman has argued that America is now 'a culture whose information, ideas and epistemology are given form by television, not by the printed word'.[16] As a result, all public discourse 'increasingly takes the form of entertainment', since entertainment is the 'supra-ideology' of TV. Politics, education and religion are, he argues, all deeply affected, and in many instances have simply followed the course taken by the advertisers—abandoning appeal to reason in favour of the emotionally persuasive power of the image. Postman's chapter on 'Teaching as an Amusing Activity' could usefully be recommended to anyone interested in teaching today. Apart from anything else, it effectively challenges the assumption that his thesis is purely American in application (a piece of insular complacency which a reading of the 1988 White Paper on the future of broadcasting ought also to dispel, for in places it plots out a scenario for the UK which has already been played out across the Atlantic). Interestingly, Postman concludes what many have found to be a deeply pessimistic book by putting his faith in education. There is, he says, only one medium of communication that, at least in theory, is capable of addressing the problem, namely the schools—although he readily admits that such a conclusion is a desperate one.

The problems posed by the persistent, ever-present images which surround us are sufficiently complex to warrant cross-curricular attention. After all, if Postman is right, the image, with its remorseless focus on the present moment, may act to jettison a historical perspective, erode ability to follow the logical steps in a reasoned argument and make us disregard that which fails to entertain. However, it is not for me to say whether teachers of English, Maths, History, Geography and so on will come to perceive this value-threatening televisual epistemology as constituting something which falls legitimately within *their* disciplinary responsibilities. But within religious education it is hard to escape the conclusion that the power of the image is a profoundly relevant phenomenon.

This is not only because of the way in which television images of religion are likely to affect pupils' perception of the subject matter, or the fact that television itself is thought by many to constitute a new and thriving pseudo-religion which has become the operative faith of millions, or the problems which those reared on images may have in understanding word-based scriptures and concepts of unpictureable deity. These are all important issues which demand our serious attention. But, in addition to them, there is a more urgent reason why image education might be given priority within religious education. If we agree that education and superstition are implacably opposed, that resistance to superstitious belief is one of the acid tests of successful religious education, indeed one of the underlying aims of education in general, then the deregulation of TV may well bring with it a powerful new challenge from the side of superstition. I am, of course, referring to the so-called 'electronic church'. The fact that this phenomenon may soon be added to the viewer's menu of choice, suggests the need for a vigorous educational response.

The term 'electronic church' refers to a certain type of religious broadcasting which has developed in America over the last few decades. Rex Humbard, Oral Roberts, Jerry Falwell, Jim & Tammy Bakker, Pat Robertson and Jimmy Swaggart are some of its best known practitioners. The programmes vary in style but are similar to the extent that they address a mass TV audience (numbered in millions) with a straightforward evangelical message, a message in which the battle between God and the devil is emphasized and conservative moral values are strongly asserted. The aptly named 'televangelists' buy time on the various TV networks, so there is an ongoing need to raise revenue simply in order to stay on air. Far from being seen as any sort of spiritual hindrance, material wealth and success are viewed by the electronic church as positive signs of God's blessing. Indeed Oral Roberts calls on God to bless his congregation in their bodies, spirits and finances.

A, perhaps *the*, priority task for the televangelists is to build up a mailing list of possible contributors to their organizations' coffers. A telephone number appears on screen during their broadcasts, and viewers are urged to phone in with a pledge, or to seek advice or prayer. Telephone 'counsellors' and sophisticated computer technology combine to allow the electronic church to build up mailing lists of those who call in, and subsequently to aim direct mailings at those thought most likely to contribute. Something of the flavour of the 'theology' involved in this process is given in Peter Horsfield's excellent book *Religious Television*.

Horsfield quotes from several mailings he received. All attempt to solicit financial contributions. One, from Rex Humbard, contains the following memorable passage:

> My heart is broken and I have not been able to eat or sleep. For today
> I had to do something which wars against every fibre in my being. I

had to take the first step to remove our programme from TV stations in your area. Eternal souls are at stake, for if our programme goes off the air there are men, women, boys and girls who will spend eternity in hell.[17]

Such computer-written 'personal' letters, going out in their thousands, have more than a hint of dishonesty about them, quite apart from their theological shortcomings. Should religious education not be geared to providing the sort of information and skills which would help to foster an intelligently critical reading of such material? (At the very least some attention needs to be given to the differences between a genuinely personal letter and the pseudo-personal production which computer and word-processor now render possible.) Should pupils who have included religious education in their syllabus of studies not have learned how to penetrate the glamour of the evangelist's glittering TV image? Are they being properly equipped to sift out the superstitious from the genuinely spiritual? Does the nature of the subject as it stands provide an adequate response to the aggressive modern manifestations of its subject matter?

Horsfield also records[18] the incredible 'Seven Lifetime Prayer Requests', offered by Pat Robertson's Christian Broadcasting Network during the construction of their new broadcasting complex. For a minimum of $100 a viewer was able to send his or her 'Seven Lifetime Prayer Requests' to CBN, who would then microfilm them and have them interred in a pillar inside the new complex, where they would be 'surrounded by prayer 24 hours a day until Jesus came back'; not to mention being surrounded by an aura of superstition reminiscent of the attitude of mind which saw nothing wrong with buying indulgences. That a sufficiently large market to make such schemes thinkable exists at all, is surely a warning sign that education in this area has not been successful (in much the same way that widespread illiteracy would suggest that English was failing to achieve its minimum goals).

It would be nice to think that the British public would somehow be immune to this sort of appeal. Viewing figures for the electronic church in America, however, give little ground for such easy optimism. Nor is our record of religious education so robust as to suggest that either the schools or the churches can be relied on to foster some sort of rugged native resistance. Of course it is by no means certain that the electronic church *will* appear on our screens, nor is the phenomenon entirely devoid of positive attributes, but the whole question of television portrayals of religion, both actual and possible, seems sufficiently important for education in this area to take urgent note of it and incorporate some form of image education into the curriculum now.

Speaking to a conference hosted by the Independent Broadcasting Authority in 1983, William Fore, one of America's foremost authorities on religious broadcasting, warned delegates of the possibility of the electronic church appearing on the British scene if deregulation became a reality: 'I can assure you,' Fore bluntly told his audience, 'that if the communication system becomes subservient to the economic marketplace, commercial religion will flourish here in patterns similar to the USA.'[19] Six years later and in light of the 1988 White Paper on the future of broadcasting,[20] communication in Britain seems to be undergoing the very process which Fore feared, namely being rendered subservient to market forces. Can we safely assume that the electronic church could never happen here?

In *Television and Religion*,[21] Fore, like Postman, stresses the important role which education has to play in equipping people to deal with the assault on values which he considers television to be mounting, both in its general output and in the programmes of the electronic church. Teaching people to understand something of the power of the image and the key cultural role which television now plays is, he believes, crucially important to educators and church leaders alike. Despite this, media education in America is still in an alarmingly embryonic form. Is the situation significantly different in Britain?

Fore told his audience in 1983[22] that the churches should become fully involved in the political process. In particular, since this is a profoundly moral and ethical issue, Fore thought that they should become involved in the process of determining the political future of mass communication, especially TV. It would be nice to think that if the churches *do* become involved here (and there are some encouraging signs that this may be happening) they might voice some support for the neglected educational dimensions of this whole debate, in particular lending their weight to the idea of incorporating an element of media education into religious education. Without education and communication no society can survive, yet the question of what, ultimately, these activities are for is one that has been curiously neglected by politicians. Perhaps the activity of the churches may help to re-focus our attention on such key areas of public concern. Whatever vision finally prevails, we can only hope that it will be one in which the important role of religious education is not forgotten.

Describing photosynthesis in a beautiful passage in *The Periodic Table*, one of those rare books which taps the literary and spiritual potential of science, Primo Levi comments on the impossibility of understanding this intricate process 'if to comprehend is the same as forming an image'.[23] Living in a television culture may sometimes lead us to over-estimate the extent to which image equals automatic understanding and make us forget that some things are simply unpictureable. If we are to escape amusing ourselves to death as Postman warns, and if we are to avoid the ignorance and intolerance which the untutored consumption of television images of religion seems likely to result in, it is important to attend now to the ways in which education can effectively address this rapidly expanding area of our experience

Note

1   This incident is recorded by Rosalind Silver in 'Pirating the Caribbean' *Media and Values*, no 32 (Summer 1985), p 8.
2   Scottish Film Council, *Media Education Curriculum Guidelines*, Glasgow: 1988, p 1.
3   Wolfgang Bartholomäus, 'Communication in the Church: Aspects of a Theological Theme', in Gregory Baum & Andrew Greely (eds), *Concilium* 1978 (a special issue on 'Communication in the Church'), p 96.
4   Marshall McLuhan, *Understanding Media*, London:1987 (Ark paperback edition), p 18. *Understanding Media* was first published in 1964.
5   William Fore, *Television and Religion*, Augsburg: 1987, p 167.
6   An important publication of the Media Action Research Centre is Ben Logan (ed), *Television Awareness Training*, Nashville: 1970. Details of the Mothers' Union media awareness programme are available from: Media Awareness Project, Mary Sumner House, 24 Tufton Street, London, SW1P 3RB.
7   The editorial address of *Media and Values* (published quarterly by the Media Action Research Centre) is: 1962: South Shenandoah, Los Angeles, CA 90034.
8   See, for example, John Pungente, *Getting Started on Media Education*, London: 1985.
9   *Media Development* is available from: World Association for Christian Communication, 357 Kennington Lane, London, SE11 5QY.
10   Robert Fisk, 'Clichés are a "real" danger to truthful news reporting', in *Action* (newsletter of the World Association for Christian Communication), vol 123 (March 1988), p 8.
11   Robert Fisk, 'Pejorative Words and Truth', an address given at the Arts Club, Dover Street, London, 12 December 1987, on the occasion of Fisk being awarded the 1987 'Valiant for Truth Media Award'. This address is reprinted in the award booklet printed by the Order of Christian Unity, who present the award each year.

12   Harvey Cox, *The Seduction of the Spirit*, New York: 1973, pp 277-8.
13   See George Steiner, 'The Retreat from the Word'. Reprinted in *Language and Silence, Essays 1958-1966*, London: 1967 and Jacques Ellul, *The Humiliation of the Word*, Michigan: 1985.
14   Marshall McLuhan, op. cit., p 305.
15   Ibid.
16   Neil Postman, *Amusing Ourselves to Death*, London: 1987, p 28.
17   Peter Horsfield, *Religious Television, The American Experience*, New York: 1984, p 32.
18   Ibid., p 34.
19   See Fore's comments in *The End of a Road* (Report of the 1983 Consultation on Religious Broadcasting), published by the IBA.
20   *Broadcasting in the 90s: Competition, Choice & Quality*, HMSO: 1988.
21   William Fore, *Television and Religion*, Augsburg: 1987.
22   See note 19 above.
23   Primo Levi, *The Periodic Table*, London: 1985. First published in 1975. (English translation by Raymond Rosenthal), p 227.

Part III

Variations on Some Important Themes

These 'variations' are attempts to explore at some length what I see as some of the most important aspects of religious education. In presenting them as 'variations' I wish to indicate clearly that they represent only one way of looking at these matters and that there are other points of view. Unless debate about religious education is kept alive, the health of the whole subject, its aims, methods and content, is bound to be adversely affected. These variations are meant to be a contribution to that debate; they ought not to be taken as attempting its conclusion. Nor ought my selection of topics be seen as an *exhaustive* presentation of the key areas of religious education; it is merely a selection. Although these pieces are rather longer than what has gone before in Parts I and II, and though I have footnoted them rather more heavily, I hope they will still be accessible to a wide range of readers. 'A Case for "Uncomfortable" Religious Education' was published in *The Month* in 1988; 'Religion, Identity and Maturity' appeared in the *British Journal of Religious Education* in 1985

15

A Case for 'Uncomfortable' Religious Education

In *The Way of All Flesh*, Samuel Butler advises us never to learn anything 'until you find you have been made uncomfortable for a good long while by not knowing it'.[1] Along similar lines, Thornton Wilder urges that 'there is no true education save in answer to urgent questions'.[2] Whilst it would be rash to build a definition of education around such comments, they do, I think, serve to highlight an aspect of the learning process which applies in a particularly important way to *religious* education. For, if we are teaching about religion in a context where the audience has *not* been made uncomfortable by having certain urgent questions brought to their attention, it is hard to see how our endeavours could be anything but unsuccessful.

A powerful clue to the nature and importance of these urgent questions comes in Aldous Huxley's *Brave New World*, a novel which envisages what a future society might be like if a careful policy of eugenics was coupled with an attempt to maximize the individual's pleasures. Into this virtually pain-free society, where everyone is purpose-bred for the work they do and where any discontentment is smoothed over by liberal use of the drug soma, comes the Savage. The Savage has been brought up in a reservation where life is still primitive and natural, so 'civilization' as Huxley imagines it comes as something of a shock to him. One of the things that puzzles him most is the fact that in this apparent Utopia people appear to be atheistic. 'Isn't it natural,' he asks, 'to feel there's a God? Isn't it natural to believe in God when you're alone—quite alone, in the night, thinking about death?'[3] To which the prompt reply is that people never are alone. In fact they are made to hate solitude and their lives are arranged so that it is almost impossible for them to have it. In a world where 'violent passion surrogate' provides the complete psychological and physiological equivalent of rage and fear, without any of their social inconveniences, where death's sting is deftly removed, or at least radically blunted, by childhood conditioning, where ageing is controlled by sophisticated medical techniques, where the potentially infirm are aborted long before birth and where the test-tube has superseded the womb, something of the whole ethos of the place is summed up when the Controller tells the Savage, 'we prefer to do things *comfortably*'.[4] Questions about God and human destiny, about the nature of right and wrong and what happens after death—questions which seem urgent from the Savage's perspective—are far too uncomfortable to be allowed any space in such a scheme.

Clearly we are a long way from the 'paradise' which Huxley portrayed. There are, however, some disturbing indications that this may be the direction in which we are moving. After all, as Peter Berger has put it in a remark quoted earlier, 'modern society has banished the night from consciousness, so far as this is possible'[5] (and, bearing the Savage's words in mind, such a banishment seems likely to be theologically significant). Likewise, to repeat John Hick's startling observation, when we realize that the average American child witnesses some 18,000 deaths on TV before the age of fourteen, it looks suspiciously as if we already have a form of death-conditioning, which may encourage us not to take our own mortality and the urgent, uncomfortable questions it poses particularly seriously.[6]

But regardless of where our civilization stands in comparison with *Brave New World*, I think it is clear that an awareness of what we might call the 'dark' side of the human situation is particularly conducive to certain urgent questions making themselves felt. Such questions, or so it seems to me, lie close to the heart of any religious outlook on the world. Yet in many of the settings where religious education is taught today, little attention is given to this more uncomfortable side of our existence. The anxieties, pains and fears which surround our vulnerable mortality tend to be glossed over and forgotten. Indeed the starker facts of our finitude seem often to receive as little mention in the classroom as the facts of our sexuality. To generalize, it is when we are alone at night thinking about death, rather than when we are, say, calculating tax-saving schemes under the bright lights of a crowded office, that many of the questions with which religions have traditionally dealt begin to dawn on us with some force. If our lives are too comfortable, is there not then a danger that we will simply fail to see with sufficient clarity that dimension of things which is of such central concern to a religious orientation? It is my contention that religious education needs quite deliberately to foster an awareness of urgent, uncomfortable questions if it is to be successful in its task of helping us towards an understanding of human religiousness.

Before much religious teaching can begin to make any sort of sense, one has to try to ensure that people see what it is getting at (which is, and this must be stressed, *quite different* from getting them to believe it.) Just as there is not much point explaining fire-drill to someone who has no concept of the various dangers posed by fire, so it can be similarly pointless introducing people to religious teachings if they have absolutely no idea what the sense of danger is against which they are being offered an antidote. If the world is seen as being somewhere secure, unmysterious, and explicable (even if some of our explanations are not yet complete), many religious teachings will simply never get off the ground—for a significant proportion of them are reliant to a great extent on the supposition that, even if people do not agree with the answer which is offered, they will at least recognize that any serious assessment of the human condition must result in the verdict of its being radically problematic. If its problematic nature is not effectively perceived to begin with, there can be no real appreciation of the possible value of any purported 'answers' or 'solutions'.

The view of it which I wish to stress here sees religion as responding to an acute awareness of human existence as something unsatisfactory, problematic, replete with urgent questions. For shorthand purposes it might be dubbed the 'question and answer' view, for it sees religious teachings very much as answering those questions which are posed by the more uncomfortable facts of human existence. Not surprisingly, then, an important part of the religious dynamic is concerned with underlining the questions, or, in other words, with making us uncomfortable. As Michael Novak writes:

> Religion is a conversion from the ordinary, given secure world into a world of nothingness, terror, risk—a world in which, nevertheless, there is a strange healing joy.[7]

Novak's striking observation serves as a useful reminder of the dark side of religion, which—like the dark side of life itself—is all too often glossed over and forgotten, so that religion comes to be seen in easy escapist terms simply as a safe haven towards which one flies from fear and insecurity. But although they do indeed offer such havens, religions also act to accentuate the sense of insecurity which desires them. The 'strange healing joy' of faith is offered in a perspective which also involves an increase in those feelings of 'nothingness, terror and risk' which fuel our sense of unease and insecurity to begin with. Unless we stress the *double* action of the religious dynamic, it is easy to view it in very simplistic terms, either as an escape for those who find it too hard to live in the spiritless world of a materialistic perspective, or as an utterly pessimistic assessment of life.

Religion offers peace of mind to heal those wounds which consciousness may come to feel more keenly precisely through an acquaintance with religious thinking. As Winston L King puts it:

> One may generalise and say that religious traditions go out of their way to paint life in its darkest colours and to stress the precarious and evil condition of human existence. Religion may be defined in this context as an awareness of the basic wrongness with the world and as the technique of dealing with that wrongness.[8]

Or, as William Ernest Hocking put it, religion may often be seen as 'the healing of a breach which religion itself has made'.[9] If religious education is to be effective, care must be taken to structure its curriculum so that the 'healing' aspect of religion is not offered until the 'breach' which it seeks to mend has been clearly perceived. There is little point in studying 'techniques of dealing with wrongness' unless the existence and nature of that 'wrongness' has first been clearly emphasized. The logic is clear: religious education must take steps to make those in its charge uncomfortable, it must make them aware of those urgent questions to which the religions of the world offer their various answering strategies.

I think there are two fundamental objections to my idea of making people 'uncomfortable' as an essential prerequisite of their religious education. *First*, it might be argued that such a process would inevitably infringe the neutrality which characterizes modern religious education as an *educational* endeavour. For if we seek to highlight those aspects of the human situation which give rise to urgent, uncomfortable questions about it, are we not, in fact, using religious education to perform one part of the double action of the religious dynamic, namely to present the 'massive religious sense of something wrong with the world'?[10] And in so doing, would we not be engaging in an *evangelical* rather than an educational endeavour?

The *second* objection to uncomfortable religious education—that is, to religious education which seeks to make people aware of those urgent questions which seem to emerge most forcefully when certain facts about the human situation are made clear—argues that such a strategy would involve frightening those whom we are seeking to educate, which is, clearly, a very serious charge, whether from a moral, educational or psychological point of view (particularly where younger children might be involved).

The famous French diarist Henri-Frédéric Amiel once remarked that 'the universe seriously studied rouses one's terror'.[11] Whilst we could, of course, cite many examples of exceptions to his generalization, there is no denying the fact that certain aspects of existence *are* frankly terrifying. Ernest Becker puts this particularly well in his psychoanalytic study, *The Denial of Death*:

> It cannot be over-stressed . . . that to see the world as it really is is devastating and terrifying . . . . I believe that those who speculate that a full apprehension of man's condition would drive him insane are . . . quite literally right. Anxiety is the result of the perception of the truth of one's condition. What does it mean to be a self-conscious animal? The idea is ludicrous if not monstrous. It means that one is food for worms. This is the terror: to have emerged from nothing, to have a name, consciousness of self, deep inner feelings, an excruciating yearning for life and self-expression—and with all this yet to die.[12]

Becker portrays the human personality much as Berger portrays human society: both are, at root, barriers against natural terror.[13]

Exposure to the stark facts of human finitude may, therefore, seem to be the very last strategy to follow in seeking to ensure a good life—which is, presumably, one of the goals of education. As a character in one of Aldous Huxley's early novels said, in interesting contrast to the Savage in *Brave New World*, 'the wise man does not think on death lest it should spoil his pleasure'.[14] Similarly, an over-preoccupation with the attendant subjects of loneliness, grief, futility, mystery, fear, despair and so on, may do little to foster peace of mind. As such, how could 'uncomfortable' religious education justify exposing those in its charge to precisely such subjects? After all, to quote Berger again, surely 'every parent who loves his child takes upon himself the representation of a universe that is ultimately trustworthy'.[15] And, acting *in loco parentis*, as the teacher is bound to do, how can we escape the extension of this duty to the classroom? Since religious education cannot *recommend* any of the religious systems of trustworthiness which it studies, has it any business to present the human situation as badly in need of some such response? Has it any business making people uncomfortable if it cannot offer them any comfort?

The *first* objection to 'uncomfortable' religious education, which accuses it of promulgating a religious outlook on the world through its focussing on urgent questions and the facts which provoke them, can, I think, be dispensed with fairly easily. In reply it must be stressed that drawing attention to facts which may be specially relevant to a religiously interpretative response, does not mean that we are bound to give credence to that response. Death, suffering, fear, a sense of the transience and vulnerability of finite existence—these are simply phenomenological facts about the human condition, which we can only deny by the acceptance of ignorance. Any *interpretative* understanding of that condition must, in the context of religious education, remain open to question, inquiry and possible acceptance or rejection. But whatever reading of the human situation we happen to endorse, it is surely imperative, and surely a primary task of religious education, that the basic alphabet which defines its major characteristics should be brought to everyone's attention. It seems to me that religious education is often in danger of assuming (quite wrongly) that all the principal existential vowels and consonants are well enough known already to proceed without further ado to the various religious readings which offer understandings of them. To call attention to the uncomfortable side of our existential alphabet is not, I would submit, some sort of covert evangelism, but a necessary preliminary to any real advancement in learning about human religiousness.

Four points need to be made in reply to the second objection:

(a) It must be emphasized that religion itself (as we saw earlier, pp 59-64, 89-90) contains a distinctly subversive element which often acts to undermine the apparent comforts and security of an ordinary outlook on the world (this is the 'nothingness, terror and risk' of Novak's characterization). If we are to continue looking at religion as a subject on the school curriculum, it is hard to see how we could avoid some mention of this element—unless we were to present a specially adapted classroom version of this area of human experience. But such bowdlerization would surely come dangerously close to distortion, censorship and indoctrination—that trinity of evils which religious education has fought so hard to overcome. An accurate presentation of religion simply demands that we go beyond the 'stories with happy endings' image of it which persists in some strains of particularly sickly religiosity. (On the subject of religious stories, it is interesting to note J D Crossan's view of parable—which is often seen as being a particularly suitable medium for children's education. 'Parable', as he puts it, 'subverts the world'.)[16]

(b) It is important to remind ourselves of the need for religious education to pay close attention to the work of developmental psychology and pitch its teaching at a point which is appropriate for the intellectual and emotional development of the child. What may be terrifying at one age may be viewed quite differently at another. Whilst it may be irresponsible to stress the dark side of the human situation at one point in a person's development, it might be irresponsible *not* to do so at another. (As Thomas Hardy said, anyone who reaches the age of thirty-five can hardly avoid recognizing the essential grimness of the human situation!)[17] In advocating any policy of uncomfortable religious education—indeed any educational policy at all—we should underwrite our curricular proposals with the clearly stated proviso: 'so long as it is appropriate from a developmental point of view'.

However, at the same time as respecting the individual's development, we should be careful not to lose sight of the fact that education lays no claim to being either easy or pain-free—those who expect it to display such characteristics are probably confusing it with entertainment. It is, after all, ignorance that education is pledged to remove—however blissful that ignorance may be in comparison to being informed. Allowing a false sense of comfort and security to develop through ignorance of the facts is surely quite unacceptable, from both a pastoral and educational point of view.

(c) We might note Bruno Bettelheim's comment about the possibly damaging consequences of *avoiding* mention of the dark side of life. Bettelheim is concerned that adult censorship of, for example, fairy-stories, where violent and unpleasant incidents are removed lest they disturb the children who read them, may in fact be quite counter-productive. The trouble with such censorship, as he explains in *The Uses of Enchantment*, is that

> children know that they are not always good; and often even when they are, they would prefer not to be. This contradicts what they are told by their parents and therefore makes the child a monster in his own eyes.[18]

Likewise Edward Robinson, defending religious education as a 'shocking business', talks of redressing the long imbalance in the subject which, in theological terms, stresses God's love to the exclusion of his power and thus provides a theistically misleading picture.

(d) This fourth and final point of reply is really an extension of what has been said above about education and the removal of ignorance. We must ask ourselves what sort of person the whole educational process is trying to produce. As John Dewey comments, 'the thing eventually at stake in any serious deliberation is . . .

what sort of person is one to become, what sort of self is in the making'.[20] Obviously there is no easy answer to such a question, but could we ever allow as a satisfactory end-product of education (religious or otherwise) someone who had never looked death in the eye and had similarly shied away from every unpleasant and troubling aspect of the human situation?

I have argued that an important task of religious education is to make sure that those in its charge are made uncomfortable by having brought to their attention certain urgent questions which stem from a clear view of the 'dark' side of the human situation. Clearly such a strategy would not be without difficulties and whether the theoretical outline I have presented here could be fleshed out successfully into the substance of credible curriculum proposals remains to be seen. If they were to have any real body, though, it seems clear that such proposals would need to contain recommendations for practical, experiential work to run alongside more traditional classroom-based activities. Bearing the Savage's words in mind, there is surely a case to be made for including on the school timetable some element of special outdoor education, tuned precisely to the needs of the religious educator. We must not ignore the 'primal curriculum' (see pp 34-40).

Only two very fundamental objections to uncomfortable religious education have been dealt with here, and no attempt has been made to anticipate in detail the host of problems which would doubtless appear as soon as the transition from theory to practice was attempted. Even so, it seems to me that in general theoretical terms the main ideas behind such a view of the subject are convincing enough to make it worthwhile to attempt such a transition and give some serious thought to the way in which a full programme of uncomfortable religious education might proceed.

Perhaps, at the end of the day, the religious educator, like the Wittgensteinian philosopher, should be seen as being in the business of 'assembling reminders for a particular purpose'.[21] In religious education, such reminders should be designed for the particular purpose of making those learning the subject feel (creatively) uncomfortable, so that they can better understand the nature of the urgent questions which lie at the heart of any religious outlook. It is no good phrasing such reminders in comfortable, unhurried terms. As Pierre Babin once observed:

> A document is apt for religious education to the extent that it expresses a deep human situation which forces one to question the meaning of his life. A document that has no shock value is of little use.[22]

Notes

1 Samuel Butler, *The Way of All Flesh*, London: 1933, p 166.
2 Thornton Wilder, *The Eighth Day*, London: 1967, p 222.
3 Aldous Huxley, *Brave New World*, Harmondsworth: 1970, p 183.
4 Ibid., p 187.
5 Peter Berger, *A Rumour of Angels, Modern Society and the Re-Discovery of the Supernatural*, Harmondsworth: 1971, p 95.
6 This statistic is quoted by John Hick in *Death and Eternal Life*, London: 1976, p 86.
7 Michael Novak, *Ascent of the Mountain, Flight of the Dove, An Invitation to Religious Studies*, New York: 1971, pp 11-12.
8 Winston L King, *Introduction to Religion, a Phenomenological Approach*, New York: 1962, p 22.
9 William Ernest Hocking, *The Meaning of God in Human Experience*, New Haven: 1928, pp 238-9.
10 Winston L King, op. cit., p 22.
11 Henri-Frédéric Amiel, *Amiel's Journal*, translated by Mrs Humphrey Ward, London: 1913, p 179 (from a journal entry dated 6 December 1870).
12 Ernest Becker, *The Denial of Death*, New York: 1973, pp 27, 87 (see also pp 59-60).
13 Peter L Berger, op. cit., p 95.
14 Aldous Huxley, *Those Barren Leaves*, London: 1925, p 281.
15 Peter L Berger, op. cit., p 75.
16 John Dominic Crossan, *The Dark Interval, Towards a Theology of Story*, Illinois: 1975, p 59.
17 Quoted without source by Richard Adams in his Introduction to Annie Dillard's *Pilgrim at Tinker Creek*, London: 1976, p 11.
18 Bruno Bettelheim, *The Uses of Enchantment*, quoted without page reference in Diane Greenwood's 'Psychology and the Use of Stories', *British Journal of Religious Education*, vol 4 no 3 (Summer 1982), p 123.
19 Edward Robinson, 'Religious Education: a Shocking Business', in John Hull (ed), *New Directions in Religious Education*, Lewes: 1982, p 90.
20 John Dewey, *Human Nature and Conduct*, New York: 1922, pp 216-17, quoted in Anselm L Strauss, *Mirrors and Masks, the Search for Identity*, London: 1977, p 43.
21 Ludwig Wittgenstein, *Philosophical Investigations*, Oxford: 1972, G E M Anscombe (tr), par 127/p 50e.
22 Pierre Babin (ed), *The Audio-Visual Man, the Media and Religious Education*, Ohio: 1970, pp 155, 159.

16

Proceeding by Story

As we saw earlier (pp 22-8), a strong case can be made for accepting stories as a good means of proceeding in religious education, simply in terms of their classroom effectiveness. Here I want to go beyond the 'tried and tested in the classroom' criterion to try to isolate some of the characteristics of stories which make them so effective in this area.

The first thing to be said is that I am using the word 'story' in a very wide sense. The narrative continuum covers an extensive area, taking in the territories of myth, legend, fable, fairy-story, folk-tale, novel, allegory and so on. To plot out the whereabouts of each particular habitat within the narrative topography would be a massive undertaking, and one which cannot begin to be started here. In its absence it is inevitable that my comments will sometimes seem most applicable to one part of the continuum, sometimes to another.

There are, I think, three main reasons why story is such a valuable means of proceeding in religious education.

(1) To begin with, stories provide an excellent methodological device for helping us to stand in someone else's shoes and see what the world looks like from there. Given that a large part of modern religious education has to do with precisely that—with trying to see how the world looks according to the teachings of Hinduism, Judaism, Christianity, Islam and so on—story has a first order importance in facilitating the shift from a self-centred outlook to one where we empathize with another self. (This does *not* mean, incidentally, that we have to *accept* that other outlook, no matter how intimately story may allow us to share its perspective.)

Interestingly, since the phenomenology of religion has had such a profound effect on the way in which present-day religious education is conducted in Britain, the basic ethos of that method has itself been likened to reading a story.[1] So when Ninian Smart makes the point that in the phenomenology of religion empathy does not equal agreement, his remarks also have a relevance for

118

religious education. Smart argues that when we are reading *The Brothers Karamazov*,

> it is not necessary to agree with Ivan in 'real life': one can still see the world from his point of view, and likewise with Alyosha. One may not in real life actually sympathize with a given character, but within the world of the novel one can have a vivid empathy.[2]

Stories allow us to stand in the thought world of the Karamazovs or of the Aborigines; they can give us access to a Hindu or Buddhist perspective; they allow us to see what an environment other than our own may be like with a detail and accuracy that is denied to a purely documentary approach; stories enable us to view past or present perspectives as if they were our own (thus, for example, some of Mary Renault's novels have been described as allowing us 'to recognize the ritual of the Cretan bull dance in the way that we recognize our own myths and communal passions'[3]). Moreover, stories act to reverse the process of abstraction which sometimes leads to a misleading picture of religion as an independent phenomenon, quite separate from the individual's other concerns, rather than as an integral and integrating aspect of a person's life.

(2) Another reason for the value of stories in religious education lies in their unique cognitive potential, which allows us to claim an importance for them over and above their usefulness in providing a pleasant, context-giving supplement to ordinary descriptive approaches. The fact is that stories can give access to areas which may *only* be accessible through story. (Thus, for example, we hear John Bowker speaking of Joseph Conrad 'struggling to explore human behaviour in ways which appear to be open to a novelist alone'.[4])

Even though we may think we know all about something, story can still add an important new dimension to our knowledge. Thus in *Reason, Truth and God*, Renford Bambrough writes:

> In reading a work of literature, as in having a new experience, we may acquire a degree of new knowledge and new understanding that is quite disproportionate to the number and importance of the new facts we learn. Some works of literature teach us that which we already know, but teach us nonetheless something that we still have need to learn.[5]

Kellenberger expresses much the same insight. Like Smart, he refers to a Russian novelist, this time to Tolstoy and his brilliant short story, *The Death of Ivan Illych*. Although in one sense the story tells us no new facts that we did not know already, *ie* that we shall die, it would be surprising if a reading of it did not add significantly to our understanding. Kellenberger writes from Ivan's point of view, but his comments apply just as much to the reader as to the protagonist:

> What he realized was not the truth of the proposition 'I shall die'. He had known all along that proposition was true. Moreover, when we try to specify Ivan's cognitive change, we find no new truth that he has realized. He has deduced no new proposition. Rather, he has more deeply realized the import of an old truth, something he cannot satisfactorily articulate as the old truth or as any new truth.[6]

The reader, like Ivan, realizes the import of an old truth more deeply, more fully. In one sense he learns nothing new, in another sense there has been a profound advancement in learning.

(3) The third reason why I think story is of such value in religious education is because of the way in which it provides a far more subtle and effective means of approaching what is descriptively elusive than a straighfoward documentary approach can offer. Since much in the religious realm falls into the category of being difficult to describe—indeed claims of ineffability, of the *impossibility* of description, litter religious literature[7]—story seems a particularly appropriate method of communication for religious education to utilize.

Moreover since story is used extensively *within* almost every religious tradition, we are not imposing a wholly foreign methodology from outside, but are rather utilizing one that already has a place in what we are studying. Apart from the use made of stories by the religious traditions themselves, to say something about what may, from a strict theological point of view, be technically 'unsayable', a further indication of the extent to which story is suitable (for the serious exploration of religious issues which would be difficult to express more directly) is, perhaps, to be found in the extent to which modern philosophy of religion proceeds by way of 'parable'—John Wisdom's story of the gardener probably being the most famous example.[8]

Applying the foregoing analysis to the story of the man in the well (see pp 26-7), we can identify at least three reasons why this story is so effective a classroom device for learning about religion.

First, in following the adventures of Samaraditya, we are encouraged to view his predicament from close quarters. It is not something that is distanced and depersonalized as a matter of no concern to us. The story form, in other words, by focussing on a person with whom everyone can identify, helps to bring home to each individual the nature of the fundamental dilemma faced by all human beings.

Second, although in one sense the story tells us nothing new—we all know that we shall suffer and die, the existence of danger and pleasure will not come as a startling revelation—at the same time it *does* help us to learn something more about such phenomena and what they mean to us. Story can exert its cognitive potential so that facts we already know about take on a new and fuller significance.

Third, within an easily managed compass, the story offers a thought-provoking perspective on life, death, salvation, suffering and so on. In other words, it manages to say something substantial about various phenomena which are not easily circumscribed in ordinary descriptive prose.

Having stressed the positive aspects of story, it is, I think, appropriate to end on a note of caution. This has been well sounded by David Ford in an interesting article on narrative in theology. One obvious danger in the concentration on narrative, he says,

> is that it can be used as a short-cut to avoid the huge problems posed by the critical thinking of many disciplines. It is easy to slip into naive acceptance of a well told story and ignore the questions that others raise at every turn.[9]

It is, in other words, all too easy to swallow a story hook, line and sinker without first looking carefully and critically at what it contains.

Although they may provide a key methodological device for allowing us to see things from the other person's point of view, we must not allow stories to prevent such points of view from being subjected to the ordinary processes of reasoned investigation; in accepting their cognitive potential in adding a new dimension to what we already know, we must not imagine that they can *replace* other modes of knowing; whilst they can prove a good means for describing what is descriptively elusive, they do not solve the considerable logical problems posed by ineffability. So long as such qualifications are kept in mind, however, there is no reason why story should not be seen and used as one of the most important vehicles of communication open to the religious educator.

Notes

1   See, for example, Ninian Smart, *The Phenomenon of Religion*, London: 1973, p 72f. The relevance of story to the phenomenology of religion is explored in some detail in my 'Phenomenology of Religion and the Art of Storytelling', *Religious Studies*, vol 23 (1987), pp 59–79.

2   Ninian Smart, op. cit., p 73.

3   Avrom Fleishman, *The English Historical Novel*, London: 1971, p 257. Mary Renault is considered by Fleishman to be 'one of the finest of current historical novelists', (p xii).

4   John Bowker, *The Sense of God*, Oxford: 1973, p 13.

5   Renford Bambrough, *Reason, Truth and God*, London: 1969, p 120.

6   J Kellenberger, 'The Ineffabilities of Mysticism', *American Philosophical Quarterly*, vol 16 (1979), p 313.

7   A selection of such claims of ineffability is contained in my 'Ineffability and Intelligibility: Towards an Understanding of the Radical Unlikeness of Religious Experience', *International Journal for Philosophy of Religion*, vol 20 (1986), pp 109–29.

8   John Wisdom's parable of the gardener, reprinted in many readers of philosophy of religion, first appeared in 'Gods', *Proceedings of the Aristotelian Society*, 1944-1945.

9   David Ford, 'Narrative in Theology', *British Journal of Religious Education*, vol 4 no 3 (Summer 1982), p 115.

17

Religious Education and World Religions

There are three commonly encountered answers to the question 'What is religious education?' These answers display a mixture of descriptive and prescriptive elements and are useful in clarifying what we mean by education in this area. The first two answers are instructive because, by and large, they characterize the popular attitude to religious education which is still found in this country. The third answer is instructive because it represents the sort of thinking which is, increasingly, being advocated by those professionally involved with the subject. Taken together, the three answers provide much of the context of opinion within which anyone involved with religious education will find themselves working. Moreover, each of the three answers suggests—in very different ways—arguments for adopting a pluralistic or 'world religions' approach to religious education.

Despite the wide range of possible meanings and motives for undertaking it, and regardless of the cogent arguments which can be advanced against such a view, I think it is clear that in a twentieth-century British context, religious education is generally held in rather low esteem. Philosophers such as Alfred North Whitehead may tell us that the essence of all education is that it be religious,[1] and educationalists such as Raymond Holley may tell us that religious education is logically central to all educational activities,[2] but for many people religious education tends to be understood in the highly restricted and dismissive sense of referring to a subject, usually of predominantly Christian concern, undertaken reluctantly at school simply because of its mandatory status and thereafter readily abandoned. As such, it has been dubbed 'the sick man of education'.[3]

The reasons for such an evaluation—which I will call the 'popular negative view' of religious education—are obviously related to the value which is put on religion in the first place, and this in its turn will, of course, be influenced, to some extent at least, by whatever form of religious education has been encountered.

The question of why an individual or a society reaches a particular valuation of religion, and the influence of religious education on such an evaluation, is clearly a very complex issue and one which cannot be explored here. We might, however, note in passing a comment made by A R Rodger in *Education and Faith in an Open Society*, which pinpoints what may be one reason why many people today seem to have rather lost interest in the whole religious realm and tend, in consequence, to be somewhat dismissive of religious education. According to Rodger's analysis there has been a tragic failure among many in our society to recognize the identity of the concerns expressed in the religions and in their own human search for meaning, value and purpose.[4] In other words, incredible though this may seem, the very basic fact that religion addresses matters of interest to anyone who shares in the human situation and asks questions about it has been missed.

At least part of the blame for this tragic failure lies squarely with those programmes of religious education which have failed to make clear the universality of religion as a matter of human concern, which have failed to get across the fundamental fact that human beings throughout history and in all parts of the world have expressed a deep interest in religious questions, although the answers they have arrived at have been multi-various. Such interest finds voice across the whole realm of human activity: in art, literature and music, as a potent social and political force, as an inspiration for all kinds of intellectual and practical work.

As we shall see, a world religions approach to religious education seems better suited than a mono-faith approach for avoiding the perpetuation of the tragic failure which does not recognize the relevance of religion to Everyman and Everywoman. For an approach which concentrates on the particularity of a specific single faith alone almost inevitably suggests that religion is a matter of interest primarily to those who belong to that group. Those who happen to be outside it, or who feel alienated from its traditional institutional forms, may conclude that they are wholly non-religious and that religion therefore holds nothing of interest or importance for them.

If we explore beneath the surface of the common opinion which sees religious education as the sick man of education, we will often find that it is being viewed so dismissively not only because it is considered irrelevant in terms of content, but also because its procedure is thought to be propagandist rather than educational. Religious education is viewed as being unfairly selective and indoctrinatory in terms of the way it handles its material. Not surprisingly, many who view religious education in these terms think that the best course of action is to adopt a policy which seeks the elimination of religious education from the school system before the contagion of its anti-educational practices spreads any further.

To the question 'What is religious education?' the popular negative view replies, 'Religious education is the sick man of education, sick because its material is irrelevant and its procedure indoctrinatory'. To such an outlook we could make various responses. We could agree without reservation and seek the elimination of religious education from the curriculum (for this is the prescriptive remedy offered by the popular negative view). This might satisfy our impatience with a persistently problematic subject, but it would be difficult to justify on any reputable educational grounds given the important part which religion plays in human experience. Or we could disagree totally and seek to defend religious education as something which is perfectly adequate—a standpoint which would inevitably leave us trying to defend practices which ought indeed to be abandoned as unhealthy. For, in places, what occurs under the heading 'religious education' *is* ill-conceived and poorly taught (the same could be said for most other subjects). The response which I would advocate to this widespread negative view of religious education is one of qualified agreement, where its diagnosis is accepted as accurate for many particular cases of religious education, but where it is argued that any sickness which the subject might suffer from stems from extrinsic, contingent and curable factors, rather than from some fatal and inevitable intrinsic flaw. Where religious education seems indoctrinatory or irrelevant, this is *not* because any attempt to educate in the area of religion must necessarily be so, but because the aims of this particular programme of religious education are misconceived or have been poorly carried out, or because the teachers concerned are poorly qualified, or because insufficient resources in terms of time and equipment have been made available.

Alongside the popular negative view of religious education stands its sibling, the 'popular *positive* view' of religious education. Here the subject is viewed as what we might call 'the good man of education', exposure to which is believed to ensure some sort of goodness on the part of the pupils. This kind of outlook makes claims of the sort that 'giving them some religion will do them some good' and sees a smattering of Bible study as a panacea for all manner of social ills. This sort of outlook on the subject provides some support in terms of raising an outcry any time it is suggested that the statutory requirement to teach religious education is abandoned, but it is by and large a passive and uncritical view

and offers little guidance concerning how religious education ought
to proceed or what it ought to contain. Its simplistic, perhaps even
superstitious, belief in the socially curative properties of religion
goes little further in terms of a prescriptive answer to the question
'What ought religious education to be?' than to say that the subject
should remain as it is (or, indeed, return to the old form of religious
instruction). As Edward Hulmes has remarked, 'it is difficult to
make progress in any direction on so calm a swell of public senti-
ment'.[5] It is also hard to accept as morally serious a view which
claims to be engaging in an activity because it promotes goodness
in some way, yet which is content that such an activity should be
given as little time as religious education generally receives. One
wonders, furthermore, what such an outlook would make of the
fact that in some respects religion at its best is subversive in relation
to much that is socially acceptable (as we saw earlier, pp 59-64, 89-
90). Whilst at its worst, religion can often be a powerful destructive
force.

The answer which the Scottish Central Committee on Religious Education (SCCORE) gives to the question 'What is religious
education?' presents a view of the subject which would make it
virtually unrecognizable to most advocates of either popular view.
As Peter Doble, Director of the York Religious Education Centre, pointed out in an interesting article in the *Times Educational
Supplement* in 1984,[6] there is a disturbingly wide gulf between
the religious education of the agreed syllabuses and the way
in which the subject is generally perceived. The existence of
such a gulf underlines the need for public relations work by
those professionally concerned with religious education in order
to communicate their thinking to society at large. According to
SCCORE, the aim of religious education is:

> To help pupils to identify the area of religion in terms of the phenom-
> ena of religion and the human experiences from which they arise; to
> enable pupils to explore the nature and meaning of existence in rela-
> tion to the questions religions pose and the answers they propose; to
> encourage pupils to develop a consistent set of beliefs, attitudes and
> practices which are the result of a personal process of growth, search
> and discovery.[7]

Now of course the discussion of what religious education is does
not stop with the SCCORE pronouncement on its aims. This is
one answer to the question of what religious education is/ought to
be and there are many who would disagree with it. However, it is
an answer which is representative of much modern thinking on religious education—similar pronouncements can be found in many of

the agreed syllabuses currently in operation in the various regions, and this sort of conception of aims is increasingly influencing what actually occurs in the schools. Such a view of religious education sees it as primarily an educational, rather than a religious, activity, in the sense that it proceeds in a descriptive rather than prescriptive manner; it is exploratory rather than ecclesiastical, more interested in teaching pupils to think about the problems than in promoting as true a particular answer to them. Such a statement of aims as that provided by SSCORE seems to demand a world religions approach to the subject.

I would like to suggest four arguments for adopting such a world religions approach, but before proceeding with them three preliminary points must be stressed.

(a) I will use the terms 'world religions', 'multi-faith' and 'pluralistic' religious education interchangeably to mean exactly the same thing: namely, an approach to the subject where the focus of attention is not fixed exclusively on any single religion and where no value judgments are made concerning the truth or falsity of particular religious outlooks. In such an approach, aspects of Hinduism, Buddhism, Judaism, Islam and so on will be considered in addition to Christianity, and no presumption will be expressed concerning which—if any—of these religions is to be preferred as true. When the various religions considered speak of God or Nirvana or Allah or Brahman, multi-faith religious education will look at what they have to say without offering an opinion as to whether God or Allah exists, or if Nirvana is an experienceable state, or whether Brahman can be accepted as an intelligible concept. The different religious outlooks will, in other words, be considered from a neutral standpoint. This is in contrast to a mono-faith approach where one religion alone is emphasized, to the virtual or total exclusion of all others, and where its teachings are presumed, and taught, to be true.

(b) It is easy to think of religious education simply as a school subject. It should be kept firmly in mind that this is an artificial restriction. Unless it is clearly seen as such we risk falling into the ridiculous position of thinking that religion and education are things which only trouble us between the ages of 5 and 16 and thereafter fade into the distance. Education and religion are, of course, more properly seen as life-long concerns. I will talk of religious education here as a school subject simply because much of the discussion focusses on this period, since it is a time when the process is of public concern and those who are involved with it are accountable to public opinion. This ought not to be taken as meaning that religious education stops at adolescence, even if its formal and visible manifestation often tends to do so. Michelangelo's admirable motto could surely serve as that of religious education too, namely: 'keep learning'. The idea of life-long religious education will be further discussed later (pp 149-60).

(c) Regardless of what verdict we might reach at the end of the day concerning multi-faith religious education, it is important to realize that in the last couple of decades there has been a massive momentum of change away from the mono-faith approach which used to characterize the subject, and towards a multi-faith approach. Commenting on the shift in emphasis from an exclusively Christian to a world religion orientation, W Owen Cole—writing in 1978—talked of 'the total re-appraisal of religious education which is now taking place'.[8] At the same time, despite this re-appraisal, a recent survey of religious education teaching in Wales revealed that a staggeringly high proportion of teachers still saw the aim of religious education as spreading the Christian faith.[9] So, as well as a gulf between popular conceptions of the subject and the views of such policy-making committees as SCCORE, there seems to be a rather alarming gulf between those who are concerned with formulating the theory of religious education and those who are charged with putting it into practice.

(1) The most straightforward argument for adopting a world religions approach to religious education suggests that it is preferable to a mono-faith approach simply because it offers a better account of the basic religious facts about the world.

According to this kind of argument, it is impossible to allow as adequate any programme of religious education which fails to inform those exposed to it about the extent and variety of human religiousness which is and has been found in the world. It is commonly suggested—in Edmund Burke's now famous phrase—that man is a 'religious animal', that somehow religion is part and parcel of being human. Thus, in his bird's-eye view of world history, Arnold Toynbee writes:

> Religion is, in fact, an intrinsic and distinctive trait of human nature. It is a human being's necessary response to the challenge of the mysteriousness of the phenomena that he encounters in virtue of his uniquely human faculty of consciousness.[10]

And Mircea Eliàde, in the first volume of his *History of Religious Ideas*, supports Toynbee's analysis. The sacred, says Eliade,

> is an element in the structure of consciousness and not a stage in the history of consciousness.[11]

But a mono-faith approach to religious education which focuses attention on a single religion alone—be it Christianity, Islam, Buddhism or whatever—is likely to miss this important point. By ignoring the extent and variety of human religiousness in favour of concentrating on one particular expression of it, it may obscure the basic fact of the universality of a spiritual dimension to human life. Multi-faith religious education, on the other hand, keeps in sight—and brings before the eyes of those it teaches —the simple fact of the extent and diversity of religion and its importance as one of the basic characteristics of human existence.

We may consider many of the forms of religion which meet our eye as we survey this area of human experience to be primitive, mistaken, absurd, even distasteful, for at first glance there is much which will jar with our accustomed outlook. But as Bishop William Beveridge put it, writing nearly 300 years ago:

> there never was any religion so barbarous and diabolical, but it was preferred before all other religions whatsoever by them that did profess it.[12]

Are we simply to ignore each profession of faith which happens to differ from our own, dismissing it as in some sense erroneous? And if we follow such a policy what is to stop others adopting it towards us?

Our species, *Homo sapiens*, appeared on the face of the globe some 100,000 years ago. Some form of religion can be traced back even to the time of our early hominid cousin, Neanderthal man. From the very dawn of history to the present, some form of religiousness has been expressed across the whole spectrum of humanity.

In such a context, to see religious belief as 'a commitment to Jesus Christ in your life',[13] and to argue that since this cannot be taught effectively the schools ought to abandon the whole endeavour of religious education, is surely to build an inevitable blindness, if not distortion, into the very definition of the subject. It is to confuse Christian education with religious education and to muddle up the role of chaplain with that of teacher.

Just as we would reject as fundamentally incomplete a course in art where painting was done in monochrome fashion with all colours but one rejected just because teachers and pupils happened to grow up in a society which had a historical preference for, say, red and among whose members this was still the most common colour preference, so we must surely likewise reject as seriously defective any course in religious education which focuses on a single religious tradition alone. Of course this is not to say that a world religions approach is in any sense anti-Christian. Christianity, an important world religion, is simply considered as one amongst others—indeed, as one which has much unique social and historical importance for anyone living in this country.

Obviously, as Ninian Smart has clearly shown, religious education must transcend the merely informative.[14] If it simply becomes a case of learning endless facts about religion it risks sacrificing understanding for the accumulation and retention of detail. And as Whitehead puts it, 'a merely well informed man is the most useless bore on God's earth'.[15] But, at the same time, there would seem to be certain fundamental religious facts about the world which are as basic to proceeding to any sort of understanding of religion as a knowledge of the spectrum of colours is to any understanding of art. Important among these basic facts is the sheer extent of human religiousness. How could this be adequately perceived by studying but a single religion?

Moreover, if we stress the universality of religion we can go a long way towards combating that part of the popular negative view of the subject which sees religion as irrelevant. For if it is truly irrelevant how can its widespread expression and influence across virtually all aspects of human activity be explained?

(2)   A second argument for world religions religious education is one which has echoes in it of the popular positive view of this subject—for it suggests that such an approach is justifiable on the grounds of its social usefulness. More precisely, it considers that a multi-faith approach is better suited to fostering social harmony than any mono-faith alternative. The argument centres around the pluralism of modern society and the pressing need for different groups to understand each other.

In a book entitled *God Has Many Names*, John Hick identified a 'new pluralism' which he suggests will be a permanent aspect of Britain's future, so that—especially in urban areas—we are going to have to live in a society which numbers Muslims, Sikhs, Hindus, Jews and other religious groups among its already Christian and post-Christian members.[16] Given this 'new pluralism' it is hard to see how we can ever return to a situation where we give our attention to a single religion alone—unless it is by the educationally dubious expedient of putting on blinkers and looking resolutely in only one direction.

It can be argued that both in terms of its method of approach *and* its content, a world religions approach to religious education combats the ignorance and intolerance on which inter-religious prejudice is founded, and thus acts in a socially useful way. If there are no assumptions made at the outset about the truth or falsity of the various religions, there is little likelihood of encouraging the attitude that others are mistaken or inferior simply because they are different; and, in investigating a range of different religious outlooks, empathy and objectivity are encouraged, *ie* the ability to imagine oneself in someone else's shoes in order to discover what it feels like to view the world from that particular perspective.

As the writer of a school textbook on comparative religion has commented:

> To teach the Christian faith only is to fail to give the modern young person a complete religious education. Our children are growing up into a racially mixed community and must learn to understand and to live peacefully with neighbours of different beliefs. Prejudice can be lessened by education; if the reasons for another's 'odd' manner of dress or 'peculiar' customs are understood they are more readily tolerated.[17]

Indeed, quite apart from working in its own subject area, religious education of a multi-faith type has in many places been a pioneer in encouraging multi-cultural studies to be adopted in schools. In both roles it can claim an active part in combating bigotry, racism and prejudice through knowledge, in a way which mono-faith religious education cannot. In short, it might be argued that multi-faith religious education is more suited to the social needs of a religiously plural planet than a mono-faith approach could ever be.

(3) My third argument for world religions religious education suggests that it offers a better approach to fundamental religious questions than a mono-faith alternative can. By 'fundamental religious questions', I mean those which ask about how human life can be meaningful in the face of the apparent accidentalness, fragility and finitude of individual existence, how any sense of purpose—beyond satisfying our material needs and avoiding as much pain as possible—can be found in our lives or perceived in the world we live in, given the utterly arbitrary and seemingly pointless occurrence of suffering and the inevitable experience of death.

Vatican Council II, in its declaration on the relation of the Catholic Church to non-Christian religions, suggests a list of questions which provide what Pietro Rossano terms 'the existential religious quest' that springs up irrepressibly in the human heart:

> What is man? What is the meaning, the purpose of life? What is the moral good and what is sin? Whence suffering, and what purpose

does it serve? Where lies the path to true happiness? What is the truth about death, judgment and retribution beyond the grave? What, finally, is the ultimate inexplicable mystery which encompasses our existence: whence do we come, and where are we going?[18]

From a quite different perspective, the writer Nikos Kazant-zakis has set out in his *Spiritual Exercises* a rather less theological but much more poetic statement of these fundamental religious questions:

> I once set out from a dark point, the womb, and now I proceed to another dark point, the grave. A power hurls me out of the dark pit and another power drags me irrevocably towards the dark pit. Where are you going? How shall you confront life and death, virtue and fear? I want to find a single justification that I may live and bear this dreadful daily spectacle of disease, of ugliness, of injustice, of death. I set my life to no other purpose.[19]

From orthodox Catholic doctrine at one extreme to a writer who professes no religion at the other, we can find the fundamental religious questions expressed. Traditionally, human beings have sought answers to such questions in a religious context, though we must remember that some non-religious outlooks, such as Marxism and humanism, may also be of some relevance here too (even if many Marxists and humanists would deny that the questions made any sense).

The persistence with which these questions have been expressed in history as a deep-seated human preoccupation would suggest, as Victor Frankl has put it, that

> man is dominated neither by the will-to-pleasure nor by the will-to-power, but by the will-to-meaning, (by) his deep-seated striving and struggle for a meaning to his existence.[20]

Indeed William Sheldon has suggested that the craving for know-ledge of the right direction, for orientation, is a deeper and more fundamental human need than sexuality, the craving for social power or the desire for possessions.[21]

If we assume that the will-to-meaning is endemic to the human situation, that certain fundamental religious questions will be of concern to everyone then, presumably, or so this argument runs, we ought to make clear the *range* of approaches and answers to these questions which are suggested by the different religions—ra-ther than focussing on any *single* approach and answer. Instead of looking solely at the outlook which Christianity offers on these questions, or what Islam, Hinduism or any other single religion has to say about them, multi-faith religious education attempts to present to its audience a range of religious teachings about the meaning and purpose of human existence, or at least to alert them to the fact that there is more than one set of answers.

As Edward Hulmes wrote in his interesting study of *Commitment and Neutrality in Religious Education*, ultimately religious education is about 'choosing sides'.[22] If this is indeed the case (and it is a debatable point), on what grounds, educational or religious, could we justify making a choice in the context of having looked at only one of the options, or from starting out on a study of the options available with the unshakeable assumption that one answer is right and all the rest are wrong?

Again, in stressing the nature of religion as addressing itself to questions of fundamental and universal human concern—and in heightening pupils' awareness of such questions—the world religions approach to religious education counters that aspect of the popular negative view of the subject which sees religion as of little or no significance. Moreover, in considering a *range* of religious outlooks on the questions which express our will-to-meaning, without pronouncing judgment on them, a world religions approach counters that aspect of the popular negative view which sees religious education as a partisan and indoctrinatory endeavour

(4) The final argument which I want to consider for adopting a world religions approach to religious education, asserts that by becoming acquainted with the teaching of faiths other than that which we personally favour, our own faith (whatever it may happen to be) becomes more mature and coherent. Conversely, if our faith develops unchallenged in a purely singular context, it is likely to lack depth and seriousness. (I am using 'faith' in a very wide sense to denote one's general outlook on life, whether it be Christian, Hindu, Marxist or nihilist.)

An analogy may help to make clear why it might be supposed that a multi-faith approach to religious education might be more conducive to the development of a serious faith-stance than a mono-faith approach. Suppose we asked two people whom they considered to be the best writer in the world and they both replied 'Tolstoy'. Suppose that we then went on to discover that one of them had never read anyone but Tolstoy, whereas the other was widely read and had considered works by Dostoevsky, Shakespeare, Joyce, Proust and so on. Would we not be more likely to see one evaluation of Tolstoy as rather more weighty than the other?

In a similar way, an assertion of faith, be it Christian, Hindu, Buddhist or Muslim, is surely more credible if it occurs in the light of a widespread knowledge of other possible outlooks on the world than if it occurs in isolation, ignorant of—or simply ignoring—other points of view.

In a sense, if someone is, say, a Hindu when they have not heard of Buddhism, Christianity, Marxism *etc*, they may be so simply by chance, rather than through any process of deliberation and evaluation; although, of course, their faith may well be a deep and critical one which will remain unchanged by any more wide-ranging religious study.

Miguel de Unamuno, one of Spain's foremost religious thinkers, remarked in his *Essays on Faith* that,

> strictly speaking in Spain today, to be a Catholic, in the vast majority of cases, scarcely means more than not to be anything else. A Catholic is a man who, having been baptized does not publicly abjure what is assumed, by a social fiction, to be his faith; he does not think about it one way or the other, either to profess it or reject it, either to take up another faith, or even to seek one.[23]

Unamuno's comment, written in 1906, holds for many countries outside Spain and for many faiths other than Catholicism. Yet if religious education is to be *educational*, it surely must seek to combat precisely this sort of unexamined, accidental, lazy faith of mere convenience. One way of doing combat is to confront the individual with alternatives which challenge the adequacy of what he already assumes or believes.

If one already holds to some religious position, the process of discovering about other faiths will increasingly provide an opportunity to review critically its various elements. As Robert McDermott has put it, 'the surest way to develop a critical attitude towards one's religious position is to travel religiously [for] sympathetic understanding of another's religious tradition reveals an alternative to every part of one's religion'.[24]

As a last comment, we might note the idea, most powerfully expressed by Wilfred Cantwell Smith, that to be a Christian or Hindu or a Muslim or whatever, *demands* recognition of and some response to the facts of religious pluralism. Thus, in a passage from his *The Meaning and End of Religion*, Cantwell Smith writes:

> Unless a Christian can contrive intelligently and spiritually to be a Christian not merely in a Christian society or in a secular society but in the world; unless a Muslim can be a Muslim in the world; unless a Buddhist can carve a satisfactory place for himself in a

world in which other intelligent, sensitive men are Christians and Muslims—unless, I say, we can together solve the intellectual and spiritual questions posed by comparative religion, I do not see how man is to be a Christian or a Muslim or a Buddhist at all.[25]

Smith's thinking is, however, very much a double-edged blade for anyone seeking to press it into service as a straightforward defence of world religions religious education; for, in *The Meaning and End of Religion*, he suggests that to think of there being entities in the world corresponding to what we term 'Christianity', 'Hinduism','Buddhism' *etc*, is utterly misleading. The practical implications of his important theory, as it affects religious education, have not yet been fully worked out.

It is, of course, quite easy to ridicule the whole idea of world religions religious education. Thus Peter Mullen delivers a blistering attack on both its content and methodology. According to Mullen:

Our method of religious education is to set up a sort of religious bazaar where the pupil can sample not only the major religions but Shamanism, Voodoo, fertility rites, astrology, numerology and the Tarot. I know a girl who did her [Certificate of Secondary Education] CSE project on witchcraft. Another was studying the various cults of unreason such as Divine Light, Guru Bhagwan Rajneesh and the Children of God. Are we supposed to think that children in the secondary school—and the less discriminating end of the intellectual range at that—are able to deal adequately with movements that are potent enough to beguile their older brothers and sisters in university?[26]

Mullen continues:

On the one hand educational experts tell us how impressionable young people are, but in the matter of religious education these same young people are expected to possess powers of judgement to which few adults aspire. Upper Juniors in Sunderland, for instance, study the life of Krishna, and the Sunderland Agreed Syllabus admits that this will require consideration of the Indus Valley civilization, the life and customs of India, some notion of reincarnation and the role of the Brahmins. Is this to be imbibed before or after morning playtime? In fact the 9 year old will have to be at it all day because he will find Muhammad and Buddha are in the syllabus as well.[27]

Mullen also criticizes what he calls the religious education teacher's 'vanishing trick' performed whenever anyone asks which, if any, of the different religions is to be preferred as true. 'Truth', says

Mullen, 'has no part in this sort of education, only opinion; and (it is thought that) the 9 year old should be "allowed to make up his own mind"'.[28]

Certainly multi-faith religious education, if it is ill-conceived and badly taught, can appear quite ridiculous. I have no doubt that there are programmes of religious education currently in operation in this country which deserve the full force of Mullen's criticisms. However, just because we can pick out bad examples does not necessarily mean that there is something intrinsically wrong with the ideas behind them and that the whole endeavour should be speedily abandoned. Were this the case we might well find ourselves abandoning every subject on the school curriculum simply because, on occasion, they are all badly taught.

Any programme of religious education which indulges in the sort of informational overkill that leads people to make such claims as—'last week we did Hinduism, next week we're doing Buddhism and this week we're doing Christianity'—is clearly quite misguided, as are curricula which focus all their attention on the eye-catching 'strange but true' or 'weird and fantastic' periphery of the religious realm. Such phenomena as witchcraft, Voodoo and what Mullen calls the 'cults of unreason' ought not to be further sensationalized by making them educationally taboo, but it would clearly be quite eccentric to focus children's attention on such things as a *central* component of their religious education.

It is easy to caricature multi-faith religious education in a highly disparaging way and proceed to condemn it as something which all but the most deluded would reject as absurd. After all, who is going to stand up to argue the case for something which asks nine year olds, from what is—at least vestigially—a Christian culture, to make up their own minds about the ontological significance of complex Hindu deities, to unravel the metaphysical niceties of Buddhism and at the same time to delve into such shady by-ways of human religiousness as witchcraft and Voodoo? Even the least imaginative can surely see the spectre of spiritual schizophrenia, devil worship and total confusion looming up by morning break.

The danger of this kind of rejection is twofold: *first*, as we have noted, because it may make us forget that, although we can ridicule a silly approach to a proposed procedure, there is no necessary reason to suppose that the procedure itself is misguided, such that *any* attempt to follow it must be regarded as inadequate. Those who wish to argue against multi-faith religious education must therefore try to ensure that their arguments are properly directed towards its theoretical substance, not focussed on the practical errors which it too would disown. *Secondly*, those who wish to *support* a multi-faith approach to religious education must guard against dismissing arguments like Mullen's simply because they seem to be misdirected, with much of their attack set against instances of what they too would agree is educationally unsound. For, in fact, beneath the colourful rhetoric of Mullen's arguments lie three vital objections which strike at the conceptual heart of world religions religious education: The *first* has to do with *the individual's readiness for religion*, the *second* with *the range of phenomena included in a world religions treatment*, and the *third* with the *methods* on which such an approach relies. Let us now briefly consider these objections in turn:

(1) The initial objection to a world religions or multi-faith approach to religious education concerns the individual's readiness for this type of work. It suggests that from a developmental point of view such an approach may be unsound.

Certainly if we misjudge the correlation between development and lesson content, the meaning of the religious material concerned is likely to be distorted or lost, possibly irretrievably. Correlating development and syllabus is thus a centrally important task for the religious education – as well as for any other—teacher, perhaps especially at the primary school stage. There is no point—in fact worse than that, it may be downright destructive—to introduce children to religious language and ideas before they are old enough to deal with them.

To put it in very simple terms, the capacity to think religiously in a reasonably mature way usually begins sometime in our teens. Some form of religious education, however, usually predates this capacity by several years. Thus at the infant, primary and perhaps even early secondary stages, it is clear that children are particularly vulnerable to non-developmental religious education; to any programme of teaching which seeks to educate them about religion regardless of the fact that certain aspects of religion, and particular ways of expressing those aspects, may be quite out of step with their level of maturity and beyond the grasp of their understanding. There is, I believe, a strong case to be made for making early childhood religious education something which is not primarily intellectual in emphasis, but which seeks rather to arouse and inspire attitudes and feelings such as love, trust, compassion, awe, a sense of mystery, reverence, and so on, in the context of which religious *ideas* may eventually come to be understood.

Clearly some of Mullen's disquiet with multi-faith religious education stems from developmental considerations. To confront a nine year old with such alien and complex religious figures as

Krishna or Buddha and expect an adult understanding of them seems simply to be misplaced. But presumably it would be misplaced in exactly the same way to ask the same child to write a comprehensive critique of Christian theodicies or to formulate his or her objections to the teleological argument for the existence of God. What has been said so far about the individual's readiness—and unreadiness—for religion applies equally to a multi- or mono-faith approach. Whether we are dealing with Moses and the burning bush, or the temptation of Buddha by Mara, or Krishna's antics with the cow-girls, we must guard against introducing such stories too soon if we wish to encourage an understanding of them as symbolic rather than literal accounts.

So far as I know, there is nothing in the work of Ronald Goldman or James Fowler, or others who have investigated the developmental side to religious education, which suggests that a world religions approach is faulted by developmental considerations. The same constraints apply to it as to a mono-faith approach, in terms of matching the subject matter to the conceptual stage which the pupils have reached. There is nothing to suggest that, on developmental grounds, the subject matter of one is preferable to that of the other.

However the debate about developmental factors finally relates to religious education, I think that champions both of mono- and multi-faith approaches must—assuming they have some concern for the welfare of those they teach—take careful note of various potential pitfalls into which *either* approach might lead the unwary teacher and the pupils in his or her charge, and *proceed carefully* in what is still an insufficiently explored area. More work needs to be done concerning individual development and, in particular, *religious* development. It may be twenty years since Goldman published *Readiness for Religion*, but we are still nowhere near ready to assert with confidence a programme of religious education which is firmly based on the individual's development. Apart from anything else, it is by no means clear what 'religious maturity' should be taken to involve, for presumably this must be the goal which a genuinely developmental programme of religious education is aiming for.

(2) The second argument against world religions religious education concerns the *range* of the phenomena it deals with. A number of points can be made under this general heading.

(a) It can be objected that the range of material covered by a multi-faith approach is bound either to be unmanageable, biased or arbitrary. It will be *unmanageable* if an attempt is made to deal with so vast a field as 'religion'—indeed even if its concern is limited to the so-called 'major world religions', there will still be so much data as to render any attempt to cover it at school level utterly superficial or quite simply impossible. Under the heading 'religion' or 'major world religions' are subsumed centuries of history, in which systems of theology, subtle philosophical debates, diverse rituals and numerous artistic expressions of faith have flourished and decayed. If this is to be taken as the syllabus which multi-faith religious education seeks to cover, then it is clearly unmanageable without some criteria of selection which would allow us to pick out particular items for consideration.

The trouble is, what criteria are there which will not render a more manageable syllabus biased or arbitrary in terms of the topics it includes and excludes? Supposing, for example, it was decided that religious education should attempt to give children some knowledge of the 'major world religions', then, to begin with, there is the problem of deciding precisely what is to fall within this category. Is Jainism a major world religion, or Shinto, or Taoism—and what of the faith of the Sikh or Parsee? Can we reasonably confine our attention to Hinduism, Buddhism, Judaism, Christianity and Islam—and, if so, on what grounds? Are we only to count living religions or ought we also to take account of such vanished giants as the belief systems of the ancient Egyptians and the Aztecs? Indeed, leaving aside the question of what to include in the category 'major world religions', what actually counts as a religion in the first place? Do we include Confucianism and Hinayana Buddhism (which is, after all, atheistic)? Could not a case be made for looking at the 'pseudo-religion' of Communism as well?

In moving beyond a single faith, a world religions approach seems to open the floodgates for an absolute deluge of possibly relevant material. With every attempt to restrict the range of material to be considered, the question is posed: is such a restriction really a tacit evaluation which does precisely what multi-faith religious education claims not to do, that is, voice an opinion concerning the relative values of the various religious outlooks? It is all very well structuring a programme of religious education in which a strictly impartial attitude is taken to the religions which are considered, but how genuine is such a neutralist standpoint if some religions are simply rejected as unworthy of mention in the first place?

Given the diversity of understandings which there are, both for the term 'religion' and concerning precisely what phenomena can be legitimately subsumed beneath such a heading, the religious educator who wants to begin impartially may simply not know where to start and what to include in his syllabus. Obviously, within the limits of available time and resources (including his skill and the pupils' ability), he cannot hope to tell his pupils *everything*. But what *should* he try to convey? Any policy of selection which is used must show how it steers a course through what would be unmanageable without it, in such a way as to pass safely between the danger, on the one hand, of being arbitrary and, on the other, of being biased. The question is, is such a 'middle way' possible?

To the criticism that he has taken on a range of subject matter which in itself will discredit his approach, the exponent of multi-faith religious education may reply in a number of ways. He might, for instance, simply point to the vast range of material covered by the heading 'Christianity' and inquire if a mono-faith approach is to be thought discredited on similar grounds, or if English literature is to be seen as unmanageable, arbitrary or biased just because it chooses some *examples* from a similarly vast field and bases its teaching on them.

After all, just because a field of interest extends further than the mental eye can see in every direction, there is no reason to suppose that every attempt to explore it will be rendered futile because it is not all-inclusive. To teach a subject which involves such a vast field of interest surely does not mean that we are automatically committed to dealing with *everything* in it. The absurdity of being comprehensive in terms of covering all the constituent phenomena which make up a particular subject area, reminds us that education is not simply a matter of gathering together, and remembering, as much 'knowledge' or 'information' as possible. As Eric Johns has stated with regard to religious education:

> During the last two decades (its) content . . . has expanded to include world religions, with the result that it has become an impossible task to state what knowledge the religiously educated person should finally possess.[29]

But this does not mean that the whole endeavour of religious education grinds to a halt in puzzlement. Far from it: the swelling of the range of information which is relevant, and the evident impossibility of dealing with it all, stresses the fact that religious education should, as Johns argues convincingly, be more concerned with fostering *skills* than with learning endless lists of names of deities, the location of holy places, key dates in religious history, and so on. The skills will, if properly taught, enable pupils to proceed into the vast area of religion/major world religion and conduct their own explorations there with some degree of confidence. As Edward Hulmes has put it, if individuals are ever to make decisions about what to believe, in a way that is neither irrational or irresponsible, 'it will be necessary for them to be made aware of some of the ways by which a personal choice can reasonably be defended'.[30]

It may well be both appealing and accurate to view religious education as a skill-inducing rather than a fact-gathering activity. But at the same time as we may acknowledge these, we must remember that there remains the task of listing precisely what these skills should be and what selection of material it is best to foster them on. In other words, the necessity of establishing clear criteria by which to *select* specific material from within the immense field of 'religion', cannot be side-stepped simply by saying that the subject is less interested in gathering facts than promoting skills. Those skills cannot work in a vacuum. In what actual religious contexts are we to show them in action? What sort of material are they best practised on?

For all protests which might be made to the contrary, world religions religious education *does* have a tendency to slip into what Peter Mullen has aptly termed a 'colourful descriptivism',[31] where basic religious issues, which require much skill if they are to be dealt with properly (such as, for example, the question of God's existence), are simply forgotten about in the fascination of looking at new and entrancing raw material.

(b) Continuing under the heading of the range of phenomena considered by multi-faith religious education, it can be objected that the sort of things this approach looks at and directs the attention of its pupils to, is simply too alien to be educationally effective. As A R Rodger puts it:

> The chance of *understanding* of religion occurring in pupils is likely to be increased if the education begins from what is familiar or, at least, readily accessible and moves out.[32]

But in a sense might multi-faith religious education be seen as 'moving out' straight away? Ninian Smart makes much the same point, though with a slightly different emphasis, when he says that:

> The study of religion may be remote and misleading if there is no point of departure from one's own cultural experience.[33]

In world religions religious education is there not a substantial risk of forgetting about a familiar point of departure and heading into the 'unknown' without laying any foundations for the understanding which will be expected of pupils?

Again, this is not an argument which seeks to criticize the whole idea of multi-faith religious education. Rather it is concerned with the question of *when* such an exercise should occur. Given the widespread condition of superficial familiarity with Christianity which is displayed by many pupils, ought they not to be encouraged to become familiar with what, in a very loose sense, they already 'know' before passing on to the utterly novel worlds of Hinduism, Buddhism and so on? And this not because of any wish to present Christianity as *the* religion, but because without some such grounding in what is familiar, their potential for understanding the new may be circumscribed. Such a process of familiarization would, however, demand all the time which is allowed to religious education on the average secondary school timetable, for there is a growing recognition that:

> a massive remedial course in Christian religion is now required in order to present young people with basic information about what Christianity is.[34]

So if a process of familiarization *is* needed at the outset of a course of religious education, it would seem that multi-faith concerns would have to be postponed beyond the years of secondary schooling.

The advocate of multi-faith religious education might reply to this sort of criticism by questioning the extent to which we can claim that children are familiar with Christianity and so should depart from there. After all, for a twentieth century child is the world of the Old or New Testament any less alien than the world of Hinduism or Buddhism? Moreover, if the familiarization process is deemed to need so much time, does it not lay itself open to the charge of indoctrination? Further, if religion is being considered as something which is concerned with certain basic existential questions, does an awareness of those questions not constitute the only sort of 'familiarization' which is needed, and can this not be done from a neutral standpoint?

(c) It might also be argued that simply by considering Hinduism, Buddhism, Christianity, Islam, and so on, in the context of their being religions, multi-faith religious education is making philosophically and theologically unwarranted assumptions. To begin with, it is suggesting that in some way they are sufficiently similar to be considered under the same heading. Yet do we have clear grounds for supposing that sufficient similarities exist between, say, Christianity and Islam to consider them both in the same conceptual breath? Even where they might appear to be similar, are such similarities more than skin-deep? Moreover, the various typological categories which are used to talk about religions—prayer, worship, sacrifice, *etc*—tend to originate within Christianity. Are we justified in transferring such a vocabulary to other faiths?

And, supposing religions can be grouped together in the first place, surely it is to misrepresent them all to present them as options or alternatives which the individual may pick and choose his way through. Is this not seriously to misrepresent the compelling power of the holy?

How is the advocate of multi-faith religious education to reply? Clearly if his approach is to be genuinely impartial it must not imply from the outset that all the religions are the same. Yet it is a simple fact of language that we refer to Hinduism, Buddhism, Christianity, Islam, and so on, as 'religions', and in so doing we surely do not assume that they are in some sense identical. In speaking of them as 'religions', is this to suggest that they are any more similar than works by Rembrandt and Mark Rothko simply by virtue of the fact that we call them both paintings? Theologically and philosophically the different religions do seem to be very different. Where, after all, is there any theological likeness between the Buddhist concept of no-self and Christian ideas on the human soul? But need the fact of there being points of phenomenological comparison between the visible manifestations of the various religions—for example, holy places, rituals, sacrifice, scriptures—necessarily act in any way to suggest *theological* similarities?

As to objections that multi-faith religious education misrepresents religion by presenting it as something which the individual can make up his own mind about after careful thought, the advocate of such an approach might surely reply that if religion is accessible to reason there seems no reason to complain; and if it is *not* accessible to reason, then religious education, along with theology, philosophy of religion and so on, may as well be abandoned.

(d) This is the final criticism which I want to consider under the 'range of phenomena' heading. It might be objected that since, historically and culturally, this is a Christian country, religious education ought to be of a mono-faith Christian variety. Furthermore, since many classrooms—especially in rural areas—are in no sense multi-cultural, the teaching of world religions in them is quite simply misplaced.

It is, of course, arguable the extent to which we can think of Britain as being a Christian country (and in historical terms we do not have to go that far back to reach a time when it definitely was not). But even supposing that it could be considered as such, it would surely be rather risky to make this the sole basis for determining what form religious education was to take. If we did so would we allow, if the climate of belief underwent a drastic change and the country became a primarily fascist one, worshipping a human führer, that the proper object of religious education would then be fascism or führer worship? In the same way, if we allow a syllabus to be entirely structured according to who is in the class, we might end up with some rather peculiar lessons of educationally dubious value. Would we ever limit the teaching of geography to the countries with which the pupils were familiar or where they came from?

(3) The third, and perhaps the most important, area of criticism which can be brought to bear on multi-faith or world religions religious education focuses on the central methodological principle on which such an approach relies. That methodological principle is *neutrality* and involves refraining from making value judgments during the course of study. In particular such a principle is adopted to enable the inquirer into religion to enter imaginatively into another's faith, to stand in their religious shoes, so to speak, and try to see and feel how the world looks from that particular point of view, rather than leaping to conclusions about it from an external judgmental perspective. Criticisms of multi-faith religious education's neutrality can take a number of forms.

(a) To begin with it is sometimes argued that it is simply *impossible* for teacher and pupil to embark on a course of religious education from a standpoint of neutrality. *Everyone* has certain thoughts and feelings about religion and it is simply being deceitful to pretend that these do not exist or that we can control them at will. A thorough-going agnosticism which might like to pose as impartiality is, in effect, no easier to 'bracket out' than a commitment to Christianity or Hinduism, Marxism or atheism. Some ideas and beliefs will, inevitably, appeal to us more than others, some will take our interest immediately, whilst others will leave us cold. How could a decision to remain neutral, to be impartial about what we encounter, alter this very basic fact that some things will appeal to us whilst others will not? Surely it is simply part and parcel of human nature to be *partial*, to be passionately committed to some things and to reject others.

The neutrality sought by the practitioner of world religions religious education does not imagine that we can wipe clean all our cherished preferences and start again from scratch, valuing nothing above anything else. It does not seek in any way to deny the existence of our various commitments. Rather it seeks to make sure that we hold to those commitments in an 'open' rather than a 'closed' manner, that our outlook on religion—whatever it might happen to be—is not dogmatically sealed against all other points of view, but is ready to consider them on their own terms and reflect on the significance of such points of view for its own outlook.

As the French diarist Henri-Frédéric Amiel wrote, 'Every life is a profession of faith, and exercises an inevitable and silent propaganda'.[35] Multi-faith religious education does not deny this inevitable profession of faith, nor does it imagine that we can be *wholly* impartial. However, just because we cannot be *completely* unbiased in our approach is no excuse for not trying to make an inquiry as value free as possible (in terms, that is, of not pre-judging the issues). There is a big difference between studying some religion whilst trying to be open-minded (which is *not* the same as being sceptical) and studying it with no attempt being made to let it break through our own ideas and 'speak for itself'.

(b) It is also sometimes claimed that a neutral presentation of the different religions (or as near to a neutral presentation as is possible) is, far from being impartial, a covert way of devaluing all religions. As John McIntyre puts it,

> the descriptive presentation of religions sets out to give no single religion any advantage over any of the others. It advocates neutrality. What passes unobserved is that thereby, such a presentation gives an immediate advantage to the non-religious, the agnostic position.[36]

Mullen too rages against this supposedly hidden bias of neutrality:

> The arrogance of that neutral point from which it is supposed pupils can be taught about all religions. The assumption of such a neutral point is itself to go beyond neutrality and to pronounce on all religions.[37]

Of course a neutral approach *could* be given this emphasis, but it is certainly not the intention behind any coherent philosophy of multi-faith religious education, where neutrality is adopted simply so as we may see clearly what is there—*not* so as it may appear in a particular evaluative light.

It is the *intention* behind adopting an objective and impartial methodology which must be subjected to scrutiny, rather than rounding on neutrality itself and declaring it to be somehow intrinsically bogus or destructive. If objectivity is simply resorted to in an effort to ensure that our own half-formed opinions do not stand between us and what we might wish to believe after thoughtful study and reflection, then surely far from passing truth by on the other side, as Mullen accuses,[38] it is more a means of helping us cross over to it safely without getting run down by whatever passing prejudice may happen to take our fancy.

Perhaps 'neutrality' is an unfortunate choice of word with which to attempt to characterize what multi-faith religious education attempts. 'Neutral' suggests in one context something clinical, inhuman and machine-like, in another something not in gear, and in yet another sense presupposes a situation of conflict from which we have decided to remain aloof. None of these connotations is particularly helpful. We would, I think, do better to follow Basil Mitchell's advice:

> Rather than aim at a neutrality which is, perhaps in theory, and certainly in practice, unattainable, we should register our commitment to conventions of free, fair, and disciplined debate.[39]

Notes

1   Alfred North Whitehead, *The Aims of Education*, London: 1970, p 23.
2   Raymond Holley, *Religious Education and Religious Understanding, an Introduction to the Philosophy of Religious Education*, London: 1978, p 169.
3   Edwin Cox, 'Religious Education: the Matter of the Subject', p 32 in Christopher Macy (ed), *Let's Teach Them Right*, London: 1969.
4   A R Rodger, *Education and Faith in an Open Society*, Edinburgh: 1982, p 67.
5   Edward Hulmes, 'Developing a Critical Faculty in Religious Education', Farmington Institute for Christian Studies, *Occasional Paper* no 9, p 2.
6   Peter Doble, 'Different Intentions in 1944 and 1984', *Times Educational Supplement*, 14 December 1984, p 37.
7   Scottish Central Committee on Religious Education, *Bulletin Two*: 'Curriculum Guidelines for Religious Education', Glasgow: 1981 par 3.2.
8   W Owen Cole writing in the Introduction to the collection of essays he edited and contributed to, *World Faiths in Education*, London: 1978, p 9.
9   'Religious Education 11–18 in Wales', report of a survey conducted

by The Welsh National Centre for Religious Education, Bangor: 1984, p 40f.

10 Arnold Toynbee, *Mankind and Mother Earth*, London & New York: 1976, p 4.

11 Mircea Eliade, *History of Religious Ideas, vol 1, from the Stone Age to the Eleusinian Mysteries*, London: 1979, pxii.

12 William Beveridge, *Private Thoughts Upon Religion*, London: 1709, article II, p 9.

13 'Vocational Education', *Times Educational Supplement*, November 1983, p 17. These remarks were made by Revd Maurice Clarke, ex-headmaster of Eltham Green comprehensive school.

14 Ninian Smart, *Secular Education and the Logic of Religion*, London: 1968, p 95.

15 Alfred North Whitehead, op. cit., London: 1970, p 1.

16 John Hick, *God Has Many Names, Britain's New Religious Pluralism*, London: 1980, pp 29, 38.

17 Jane Bradshaw, *Eight Religions in Britain*, London: 1979, Preface.

18 Quoted by Pietro Rossano in 'Christ's Lordship and Religious Pluralism in Roman Catholic Perspective', in Gerald H Anderson & Thomas F Stransky (eds), *Christ's Lordship and Religious Pluralism*, New York: 1981, p 96.

19 Nikos Kazantzakis, *The Saviours of God, Spiritual Exercises*, New York: 1960 p 72f.

20 Quoted by Huston Smith in *Condemned to Meaning*, New York: 1965, p 21.

21 Quoted by Huston Smith in *The Purposes of Higher Education*, New York: 1955, p 36.

22 Edward Hulmes, *Commitment and Neutrality in Religious Education*, London: 1979, p 103.

23 Miguel de Unamuno, *The Agony of Christianity and Essays on Faith*, London: 1974 (the essay from which I quote was first published in 1906), pp 172-3.

24 Robert McDermott, 'Religion as an Academic Discipline, *Cross Currents*, vol 18 (1968), p 29

25 Wilfred Cantwell Smith, *The Meaning and End of Religion*, London: 1978, p 11.

26 Peter Mullen, 'Passing Truth by on the Other Side', *Times Educational Supplement*, 4 May 1984, pp 22-3.

27 Ibid.

28 Ibid.

29 Eric Johns, 'Some Skills for Religious Education', the *British Journal of Religious Education*, vol 5 no 2 (Spring 1983), p 69

30 Edward Hulmes, 'Developing a Critical Faculty in Religious Education', Farmington Institute for Christian Studies, *Occasional Paper* no 9.

31 Peter Mullen, *Thinking About Religion*, London: 1981, p 11.

32 A R Rodger, *Education and Faith in the Open Society*, Edinburgh: 1982, p 111.

33   Ninian Smart, 'The Comparative Study of Religion in Schools', in Christopher Macy (ed) *Let's Teach Them Right*, London: 1969, p 64.

34   Edward Hulmes, *Commitment and Neutrality in Religious Education*, London: 1979, p 92.

35   Henri-Frédéric Amiel, *Journal Intime*, translated and with an introduction and notes by Mrs Humphrey Ward, London: 1913, p 24. (Amiel's entry for 2 May 1852).

36   John McIntyre, 'Multi-Culture and Multi-Faith Societies: Some Examinable Assumptions', Farmington Institute for Christian Studies, *Occasional Paper* no 3.

37   Peter Mullen, 'Passing Truth by on the Other Side', *Times Educational Supplement*, 4 May 1984.

38   Ibid.

39   Basil Mitchell, *Neutrality and Commitment*, Oxford: 1968, p 22.

18

Religion, Identity and Maturity

The idea of some sort of psychological rationale for religious education, which seeks to present it with reference to the individual's growth, is not a new one. Goldman's seminal *Readiness for Religion* was, after all, put forward precisely as a basis for *developmental* religious education. Much of the emphasis in thinking about this psychological dimension of the subject has been on ensuring that, at any given point, the content of a religious education syllabus matches the stage of intellectual/emotional maturity which pupils have reached, so that we do not, for example, confront the intuitive or pre-operational religious thinking of the young child with issues which require a more sophisticated cognitive outlook for their proper understanding. As Goldman put it, 'the greatest danger for the infant pupil is that of acquiring a religious vocabulary which has no conceptual substance'.[1] If we misjudge the correlation between development and lesson content, the meaning of the religious material concerned is likely to be distorted or lost, possibly irretrievably. Correlating development and syllabus is thus an important task and one on which much work still needs to be done—perhaps especially in light of the world religions approach which increasingly characterizes the subject.[2]

In seeking to suggest some links which might be forged between Erik Erikson's model of each individual's path towards maturity and the teaching of religious education, I am not primarily concerned with the question of how exactly we should match lesson content with intellectual/emotional development, although I hope that some useful reference points for this vital correlation may, in fact, emerge. My main aim is, rather, to tease out from Erikson's developmental theory a framework of possible goals in relation to which our conception of religious education might be radically expanded, and to show, with particular reference to adolescence, the paradoxical nature of the relationship between religion and identity.

In his widely influential *Childhood and Society*, Erik Erikson presents a comprehensive theory of human development. He

149

identifies eight critical points spaced out along the individual's path towards maturity. At each of these points we are faced with the possibility of a positive or negative developmental outcome, one taking us further towards maturity, the other anchoring us to some aspect of immaturity. *Full* maturity is only possible if we are successful in escaping from all of the potential pitfalls with which these critical points present us. Chapter 7 of *Childhood and Society* discusses the 'eight ages of man' in detail and I will not attempt to repeat or summarize Erikson's presentation here, beyond giving the very barest reminder of his theory. His account is sufficiently lucid and compelling to make extensive paraphrases of it redundant.

In terms of the positive or negative outcomes which present the individual with eight fundamental tensions, each one of which he must attempt to resolve in a way that is healthy, non-neurotic and non-destructive for the psyche, Erikson's ages of man are:

1   basic trust *versus* basic mistrust
2   autonomy *versus* shame and doubt
3   initiative *versus* guilt
4   industry *versus* inferiority
5   identity *versus* role confusion
6   intimacy *versus* isolation
7   generativity *versus* stagnation
8   ego integrity *versus* despair

The categories of possible outcome in these eight ages of man are presented as senses which pervade surface and depth, consciousness and unconsciousness. They are, according to Erikson, a mixture of ways of experiencing, ways of behaving and unconscious inner states—and are thus best examined at one point by introspection, at another by objective observation, and at another by psychoanalytic tests and analysis.

Erikson's developmental model stretches from the first positive achievement on the path to maturity, the infant's willingness to let the mother out of sight without undue anxiety or rage 'because she has become an inner certainty as well as an outer predictability',[3] to the final acceptance of one's life—however imperfect it may be perceived to be—as 'something that had to be',[4] rather than as something which could admit of fantasy alternatives. The theory is drawn into a pleasing and plausible 'circularity' by a comment of Erikson's which serves to link the first and final age:

> it seems possible to paraphrase the relation of adult integrity and infantile trust by saying that healthy children will not fear life if their elders have integrity enough not to fear death.[5]

This remark has, I think, a particularly questioning resonance for the teacher of religious education.

The relationship between the goals of the various ages which Erikson identifies is further revealed when we realize that

> the strength acquired at any stage is tested by the necessity to transcend it in such a way that the individual can take chances in the next stage with what was most vulnerably precious in the previous one. Thus the young adult, emerging from the search for and the insistence on identity, is eager and willing to fuse his identity with that of others.[6]

In other words, he is ready to try for the 'goal' of intimacy. In a moment I will look more closely at how the tension between identity and role confusion arises in adolescence, and how the possible role which religious education might play, in aiding the successful resolution of this tension, gives rise to perplexing questions about the relationship between religion and identity. First, though, I want to suggest how Erikson's thinking might provide the basis for a somewhat more extended vision of what religious education is—or ought—to be than is normally suggested by thinking of it simply in terms of a school subject.

Although Erikson is concerned with *childhood* and society, his theory of human development provides a model of progressive maturation which stretches from infancy to old age. In seeking to link its insights to the teaching of religious education we are thus provided with a potential mandate for *lifelong* religious education. Such a mandate would seem to be more in keeping with the underlying ethos of the subject than a purely school-based endeavour could ever hope to be. Since Erikson's theory of development identifies specific goals for stages in life, from its very beginning to its end, it suggests a programme of religious education which extends well before the primary and long after the secondary curriculum. For unless we wish to 'tie' religion solely to some specific part of life, which would be to risk, seeing it as something immature or static, we must presumably see it as having some role in dealing with each of the various pressure points of maturity which the eight ages of man locate.

Unlike some theories of development, Erikson's eight ages provide an unbroken continuum of human growth which does not allow us simply to equate maturity with biological completion at puberty. Unless, therefore, we wish to equate religious maturity with merely physiological factors, education concerning religion ought surely to be a *continuing* process. If religious education could offer no potential for aiding the individual's drive to reach those developmental goals which are presented by Erikson as defini- tive of the whole and healthy person, then (assuming his theory to be accurate) unless we accepted a complete divorce between psychological and religious development we would surely have to to question both the entitlement of religious education to a place on the curriculum and its competence in handling the holy, which is also concerned with human completeness.

Whether or not religious education could be planned sequent- ially so that it would attempt to foster in turn each of the eight positive developmental goals at the time when individuals are faced with these critical points in their biographies, is hard to tell. The idea of pre-school religious education focussing on trust and autonomy, primary school religious education focussing on initia- tive and industry, secondary school religious education focussing on identity and intimacy, and post-school religious education on generativity and ego integrity, whilst combating mistrust, guilt, shame, and so on, does, however, have a certain appeal on at least three separate counts.

(1) It would, as I have suggested, extend the range of the individual's exposure to the subject in a way which is surely con- sonant with the nature both of religion and of education. Such a radical extension would certainly stand as an effective counter- weight against any trivializing of religion which might come about in the minds of those hitherto exposed to learning about it solely within the confines of one forty minute period per week. (How could it appear as *other* than trivial if that is all the time allotted to it in the course of a life?)

(2) It would provide a possible way of harmoniously fusing religious, moral and social education in pursuing common object- ives, which would surely be more satisfactory than the uneasy and ill-defined relationship which currently exists between them. Moreover, such a joint effort would allow these subjects to mirror the overlap of concern which exists between religion, morality and society, rather than suggesting three discrete areas of interest by a simplistic compartmentalization.

(3) Trust, autonomy, initiative, industry, and so on, might, perhaps, provide a substantial clue towards finding some method for selecting those elements in any religious teaching which are *intrinsically* valuable, at least from the point of view of a developmental perspective, regardless of the truth or falsity of the ontological matrix in which they are embedded. Such elements might be suitable for inclusion in a neutral programme of religious

education which seeks to offer no opinion on the truth or falsity of religious statements about how thing are. This sort of method of selection might also go some way towards solving the problem of what range of subject matter religious education should attempt to cover.

Clearly many questions are raised by a proposal to extend religious education so radically, by means of reference to an Eriksonian framework. Can Erikson's theory of development be accepted as accurate in the first place? Can we tie a programme of religious education to the eight ages of man and still claim to be engaged in a neutral activity? How, practically speaking, could the criteria suggested by Erikson's model be used to select material for the classroom? Would a religious education curriculum designed with close reference to the eight positive parameters of maturity suggested by Erikson's model, effectively cover the full range of religious phenomena with which we would expect religious education to deal?

Such questions map out a course of extensive study and research which would require the co-operation of psychologists, educationalists, theologians and philosophers. However, despite the volume of work which would need to be done before endorsing an Eriksonian model of religious education, it is clear that Erikson's theory has at least a first-order plausibility in suggesting goals for a radically extended programme of education in this area and, as such, qualifies as a topic deserving further attention.

Erikson's presentation of the critical tension faced by the adolescent as being that strung out between a sense of identity and the threat of its obverse, role confusion, is one which finds support in the thinking of many psychologists of adolescence. Arthur T Jersild, for example, points precisely to the issue of identity as what constitutes the basic 'storm and stress' which traditionally accompanies adolescence. Jersild's thinking is particularly relevant to our present concern for two reasons. *First*, he is careful to stress that 'there is much of the adolescent left in all of us'[7] whatever chronological age we may happen to have reached, and that anything which helps a person to understand adolescence therefore 'gives him a better understanding of the kind of person he now is'.[8] This acts as a useful counterbalance to the risk of seeing the eight ages of man as a series of simplistically successive steps which jettison themselves as the individual ascends them, rather than as aspects of the human psyche which may have simultaneous and inter-mixed expression at almost any chronological age. *Second*, Jersild's definition of final maturity in terms of developing a sense of compassion is one which I think provides a further psychological goal for the whole endeavour of a radically extended religious education.[9]

The so-called 'normative crisis' of adolescence[10] stems largely from the biological changes attendant on puberty and the societal attitudes towards an individual at this stage of development. In a sense the adolescent's whole picture of him or her self is rudely shattered. The old image of self as child becomes redundant, yet at the same time there is no immediate entry into adulthood. Instead, the individual seems momentarily caught in a disturbing psycho-social and sexual no man's land where any step forward seems to require both serious choice and responsibility, neither of which things the adolescent feels ready to undertake. The whole period of adolescence has been aptly described by D W Winnicott as a 'doldrums' area.[11] It is within such an area that the adolescent is faced with the risk of role confusion—of not knowing who he is, or what he wants to be, or what he ought to do. The tension of such potentially damaging uncertainty may only be safely resolved by his arriving at a firm sense of identity.

If we take adolescence as running roughly from the age of twelve until the late teens or early twenties, and if we accept identity as one of the fundamental concerns of religion, then, supposing that the view of adolescence offered by Erikson and Jersild is an accurate one, it is clear that some of the deepest concerns of the secondary school pupil run parallel to issues towards which much religious thought has been directed. It seems plain that during this particular developmental stage there is thus a strong case to be made for religious education focussing its attention precisely on what 'speaks to' the hurdle of maturity/immaturity which is being encountered. In this way religious education may strive in assisting at a successful resolution of the tension between identity and role confusion, thus confirming the relevance of religion as an aspect of the maturity which is being sought.

The idea of using religious education as a means of fostering maturity by focussing its presentation of religion on the particular developmental goals identified by Erikson is, I think, an appealing one. The idea gains considerable credence from an examination of the work of James Fowler, who has suggested that in contrast to Piaget and Kohlberg—whose work sheds interesting light on the structures of faith at different stages in development—Erikson helps us to focus on the *functional* aspect of faith, the expected existential issues with which it must help people cope at whatever structural stage across the life cycle.[12]

The eight hurdles on the path to maturity which Erikson identifies may, in other words, be seen as the major sequence of challenges, in response to which a developing faith defines and refines itself. Granted, it may not be easy to envisage straight away how religious education would address itself to industry, initiative and so on in concrete terms of actual lesson content; sometimes moral or social education seem more suited to the task. But with reference to adolescence and the tension between identity and role confusion, there would seem to be no particular reason why clear curricular proposals could not be worked out which would make use of religion, with its fundamental concern with the questions 'who am I?' and 'how ought I to live?', as a means of nurture/education geared towards effecting the desired developmental outcome.

However, although religious education might, at first sight, seem to provide a significant means of helping to get over this particular developmental hurdle, such an intended strategy raises two serious questions about the relationship between religion and a sense of identity.

(1) To begin with, if religious education is to remain in the context of a world religions approach (and it is difficult to see how it could revert to a mono-faith base at this stage without losing a great deal of credibility), then it follows that it will introduce *many* answers to the questions 'who am I?' and 'how ought I to live?', rather than a single one. In a sense, as I have suggested earlier, such religious education provides a *hall* of mirrors rather than a single image, and the many reflections to which it gives access may serve to further fragment and confuse the adolescent's sense of identity, instead of helping it to develop and cohere. It seems likely that a good case could be made for arguing that exposure to a *variety* of self images actually helps to foster a more informed, tolerant and understanding personality at the end of the day, and that it avoids the risk of allowing one-dimensional masks of inherited tradition, considered dogmatically and in isolation, to take the place of any more sophisticated sense of our own and others' identities. However, it seems important to bear in mind the possibility that in terms of identity, the presentation of information about many religions would seem to involve a risk of confusion, whilst in terms of a developing faith it might act to foster precisely that variety of polytheism which Fowler has identified.[13] Moreover, if—as Erikson suggests—a confusion of values results from the

absence of any sort of particular ideological commitment, such as might be fostered by an encounter with religious pluralism, then it is worth reminding ourselves of his contention that this

> can be specifically dangerous to some but . . . on a large scale it is surely dangerous to the fabric of society.[14]

In other words, identity confusion may have socially, as well as individually, undesirable consequences. With these possibilities in mind we are surely forced to consider very carefully in what way—if any—religious pluralism can be suitably introduced to the adolescent consciousness. Perhaps at this point it is useful to remember that religious education can be viewed as much as an encourager of certain *skills* as a purveyor of possibly confusing information. This insight can, I think, provide a valuable clue as to how an acquaintance with several religions might foster rather than frustrate the development of a mature faith and a resilient sense of identity.

(2) As we saw earlier (pp 59-64, 89-90), there is a very real sense in which religion has a subversive and destructive side. Within that disturbing world of nothingness and terror which Novak identified as belonging to religion, he also admits the existence of a 'strange healing joy'.[15] But can the religious educator guarantee that the pupils in his charge will find it? If not, ought he to expose them to it in the first place? There seems little doubt that religion is disruptive of many ordinary certainties and critical of many models of identity thought to be adequate, or even admirable, by society at large.

Is religion, then, even if it were to be considered in a singular context, a suitable subject for adolescents in the midst of an identity crisis? In a sense, when it comes to identity, religion acts to foster a pervasive and effective sense of role *absurdity*, if not role confusion, prior to the presentation of a deeper sense of meaningful identity. This religious trend is well summed up by Heinrich Zimmer in an account of what we might call the Indian experience of identity *v* role confusion (for would it not be possible to view the Upanishads, at least in part, as expressing India's spiritual adolescence?):

> What is man really, behind and beyond all the marks, costumes, implements and activities that denote his civil and religious status? What being is it that underlies, supports, and animates all the states and changes of his life's shadow-like becoming? The anonymities of the forces of nature that operate within him; the curious performances, successful or unsuccessful, upon which his social character depends; the landscape and life incidental to his time and place of

birth; the materials that pass through and constitute for a time his body, charm his fancy, and animate his imagination: none of these can be said to be the self.[16]

In other words, such a religious outlook queries the adequacy of any of our ordinary reference points for affirming who we are. The identity-destruction which religions seem bound to foster, albeit en route to the deeper senses of being which they claim to perceive underlying our more everyday concepts of identity, does have a certain intellectual excitement about it and is doubtless a necessary stage in reaching any sort of religious maturity. But is religious maturity necessarily compatible either with psychological canons of normality or with socially approved modes of behaviour? Does the psychological concept of a whole and healthy person tally with religious concepts of a holy person, and can the demands of certain religious insights be met within the ordinary social context in which religious education is customarily based? Erikson sets *Homo religiosus* apart from ordinary man in terms of the former's *lifelong*, as opposed to eventual, struggle with the integrity crisis,[17] and Fowler has pointed out that those few individuals who reach the most mature of the stages of faith which he identifies (the universalizing faith of stage six) are, as he puts it,

> often experienced as subversive of the structures (including religious structures) by which we sustain our individual and corporate survival, security and significance.[18]

In consequence,

> many persons at this stage die at the hands of those whom they hope to change.[19]

To which set of values—religious, social, or psychological—do we appeal in trying to decide to what extent, in an educational setting, young people ought to be brought into contact with what might be termed the negative, disturbing and dangerous (albeit perhaps *eventually* positive and reassuring, maybe even saving) side of religion? Is there not a clear sense in which religion is destructive of any ordinary sense of identity and powerfully *anti*-social, or at least set dead against some particular parts of society's fabric? These questions raise seriously disconcerting doubts, not only about the specific issue of how/if Erikson's developmental model may be used as a point of reference for religious education, when religion seems to go beyond the bounds of ordinary developmental goals; but also about the more general issue of precisely what religious education is attempting to achieve and, that endlessly recurring koan-like question, exactly how it stands in relation to its highly potent subject matter.

Can either religion's terror and risk, or its strange healing joy, be introduced responsibly and effectively in a course of religious education with a clear sense of what the purpose behind such an introduction is? In particular, can these dimensions of religion be utilized to help the adolescent, or his younger or older fellow seekers, find a mature faith and a positive sense of identity which will provide a secure and stable personality base, or will they simply complicate the whole issue? One thing seems clear, if religious education is conceived of in limited terms as a process which is given a minimal amount of time in school and is henceforth abandoned, then there is little chance of it fulfilling any particularly significant role in relation to identity or maturity, however we might define these two key developmental concepts.

One of the paradoxes of religion is that it offers both fundamental certainty and uncertainty, a rich source of meaning and a formidable vision of what is meaningless. In order to set the stage upon which to present its sense-giving outlooks on the human condition, it first points to the features of that condition which call out for its perspective in the first place. It shows the meaninglessness, uncertainty, incompleteness and absurdity of life considered adequate without some sort of transcendent dimension. Religion, as Hocking put it, is often 'the healing of a breach which religion itself has made'.[20]

To what extent and in what manner ought a programme of religious education to present to those exposed to it what Winston L King has called 'the massive religious sense of something wrong with the world'?[21] This sense of wrongness, which must be appreciated before the meaning of the religious alternatives can come properly into focus, casts a shadow of absurdity, uncertainty, futility and flawedness on to much of what we ordinarily take for granted as adequate, including our sense of identity.

Perhaps an answer here depends on precisely that issue which present-day religious education circumvents so cautiously and is understandably reluctant to come to grips with: namely, whether or not the religious sense of meaning, the offered antidote to the ills of non-religious being, is at the end of the day, *accurate*. King, as we have seen, defines religion as

> the awareness of a basic wrongness with the world and. . .the technique of dealing with that wrongness.[22]

But is the awareness thus fostered by religion one that would help or hinder us in our progress towards a socially acceptable mode of maturity? And are the techniques on offer effective ones? For if they are not, might not the sense of wrongness with the world highlighted (or indeed initiated) by religion simply lead us towards that eighth and final state of immaturity, *ie* despair?

It is obvious that maturity must be one of the principal goals of education. Precisely what maturity consists of and what role religion has to play in it is, I think, one of the most important questions to emerge from all our foregoing deliberations. As Fowler observes,

> careful theological work is required in a faith tradition to determine the normative images of adulthood which that tradition envisions.[23]

If, after such work, we discover that different traditions have radically different models of maturity in mind, or if those models systematically conflict with a psychological analysis of development, such as that contained in Erikson's eight ages of man, then the task of formulating any effective programme of non-partisan religious education will be considerably complicated. If, on the other hand, we can arrive at some commonly agreed model of what it means to be mature, then we would be ready to begin mapping out a programme of religious education which deliberately attended to each facet of the development necessary to reach that maturity. It is surely almost inconceivable that such a mapping would suggest an educational journey that was anything other than a continuing and lifelong process.

Notes

1   Ronald Goldman, *Religious Thinking from Childhood to Adolescence*, London: 1964, p 232. Similarly, James W Fowler (*Stages of Faith, the Psychology of Human Development and the Quest for Meaning*, San Francisco: 1981, p 132) draws attention to the risk of precocious identity formation if children are exposed at an early age to insistent fundamentalist literalism. Such premature voicing of adult-endorsed opinion is surely very much a case of words without concepts, indeed with very little sense at all attached. When young people, either through choice or undue influence, take on the values and lifestyles of their parents without questioning, they enter an identity status which James Marcia has aptly termed 'foreclosure'. (Quoted in Helen L Bee & Sandra K Mitchell, *The Developing Person*, New York: 1980, p 611.)

2   It is, for example, difficult to know whether—or when—to include Buddhism in the religious education curriculum when the secretary of the British Mahabodhi Society (founded by Angarika Dharmapala in 1926) asks of teaching Buddhism in the classroom, 'is it really worth the effort when religiousness or spiritual awareness at a rational,

intelligent level only occurs at the 6th form stage, if then?' Personal communication with Russell Webb, 30 October 1982.

3   Erik H Erikson, *Childhood and Society*, St Albans: 1977 (1950), p 222.

4   Ibid., p 241.

5   Ibid., p 242.

6   Ibid., p 237.

7   Arthur T Jersild, *The Psychology of Adolescence*, New York: 1963, p 5.

8   Ibid.

9   Towards the end of *The Psychology of Adolescence* Jersild notes that 'much of what has been said in this and earlier chapters suggests that compassion is the ultimate embodiment of emotional maturity'. See p 405 for the definition of compassion which follows this claim.

10   Many would disagree with the view of Erikson *et al.* that adolescence is a normative crisis whose stresses and tensions are an unavoidable part of growing up. Margaret Mead has, for example, argued convincingly that the 'storm and stress' aspect of adolescence is due to factors unique to a modern industrialized society and that they do not find invariable expression in adolescents from every society. See her *Growing up in New Guinea*, London: 1930, and *Coming of Age in Samoa*, London: 1943.

11   D W Winnicott, *The Family and Individual Development*, London: 1965, p 84.

12   James W Fowler, *Stages of Faith, the Psychology of Human Development and the Quest for Meaning*, San Francisco: 1981, p 109. Note that for Fowler 'faith is not always religious in its content or context' (p 4). He defines faith as 'our way of finding coherence in and giving meaning to the multiple forces and relations that make up our lives' (p 4). Moreover, 'the opposite of faith is nihilism (rather than doubt), the inability to imagine any transcendent environment and despair about the possibility of even negative meaning' (p 31).

13   Ibid., p 19f.

14   Erik H Erikson, op. cit., p 188.

15   Michael Novak, *Ascent of the Mountain, Flight of the Dove, An Invitation to Religious Studies*, New York: 1978, pp 11-12.

16   Heinrich Zimmer, *Philosophies of India*, New York: 1951, p 159.

17   See Erik H Erikson, *Young Man Luther, A Study in Psychoanalysis and History*, London: 1972 (1958), pp 254-5.

18   James W Fowler, Robin W Lovin *et al.*, *Trajectories in Faith*, Five Life Stories, Nashville: 1980, p 31.

19   Ibid.

20   William Ernest Hocking, *The Meaning of God in Human Experience*, New Haven: 1928, p 238.

21   Winston L King, *Introduction to Religion, A Phenomenological Approach*, New York: 1968, p 22.

22   Ibid.

23   James W Fowler, *Stages of Faith*, p 294.

Afterword

H G Wells once remarked that human history has become more and more a race between education and catastrophe.[1] It often seems today that catastrophe is miles out ahead, chest almost breaking the fragile tape which separates mere probability from what happens. Meanwhile education has scarcely left the starting blocks, or else has stopped—after an initial burst of energy and enthusiasm—to tie a shoe-lace, recover from a cut-back, plan a module, negotiate a wage settlement, or follow some other diversion from its main business, which is to win. Doubtless the causes for catastrophe's apparent lead and education's lagging far behind are both legion and complex. But at least one of them is quite simple and, at least in theory, easy enough to remedy: namely, the lack of education about education.

It is an interesting (although often depressing) exercise to ask those who are undergoing it in the formal public setting of school or university what they think their education is all about and what it is meant to achieve. The most common answers I have come across, whether from pupils or undergraduates, provide a set of variations on the theme: '*education = qualifications = employment*'. Learning is promptly reduced to certification; avoidance of unemployment, rather than the removal of ignorance, provides the *raison d'être* for acquiring knowledge.

Alas, in the current job-market in Britain, this common utilitarian equation seems often not to hold. It should come as no surprise, then, that those who evaluate education according to its terms are, increasingly, coming to think that education has little or no value; that it is, in fact, a pointless undertaking given its frequent failure to secure paid employment. Where such a conclusion is reached before the age of educational consent, when the individual may decide for himself whether to continue with his studies or not, it is guaranteed to lead to an attitude of truculence, if not outright disruption, whose negative force will seep like a paralysing poison through any attempt at group learning. That the attitude is understandable is unlikely to make it any easier

161

to bear in a classroom situation. Such an understanding may, however, suggest strategies for preventing its outbreak in fresh cases.

Where, in the course of the average school curriculum, is there any place reserved for explaining the intrinsic value and purpose of education, as distinct from its vocational usefulness? We can no longer suppose—if indeed we ever could—that this is so obviously self-evident as not to need some attention. Very seldom does there seem to be any self-conscious effort *to educate about education*— yet, in a very real sense, unless such a task has been successfully performed, every subject on the timetable risks failure through a quite needless missing of the point by those who are being taught. There is a high risk of the seeds of learning falling on unreceptive ground, indeed of their being actively rejected, if pupils' minds are not opened to the value of the educational process and all the diverse germination it can offer. Unless the uneducated life is clearly seen as far less worth living than its educated alternative, quite regardless of any outcome measured by the criterion of employment, how can we hope for an attitude in pupils which is much more than that of mere acquiescence?

It is easier to see the value of studying some subjects than studying others, and inevitably, as specialization increases, the reasons behind undertaking any work tend to recede. Thus it is easier to see the value of, say, home economics than some of the more abstract areas of mathematics. Likewise, whilst the study of life (the general brief of biology) may be quite intelligible to everyone, it is more difficult to appreciate the motivation behind some of the more esoteric avenues of inquiry opened up by, for example, electron microscopy. Specialization is the price we pay for the advancement of learning. It is a price because it can cost us that sense of purpose which explains why we wanted to learn something in the first place. Perhaps one of the most important skills of the good teacher is to be able to mediate effectively between the knowledge which specialized inquiry yields and the natural curiosity which lies at the root of all inquiry, but which can be killed off if it is exposed too soon, or in the wrong concentration, to the upper branches of the tree of knowledge. The price of specialization is not something which can be paid in the classroom without the risk of bankrupting the whole educational system.

As a teacher of religious education I suppose I have been exposed more often than many of my colleagues in other subjects to the rejection of my work as useless. 'What's the point in doing religious education, it can't get you a job?' 'Why do I have to come to these classes, I don't want to be a minister?' 'Religious education's useless, why do we have to waste our time with it?' Such questions as these must be a familiar refrain to many religious education teachers' ears. Some of the ill-feeling which religious education tends to encounter can, of course, be put down to the only semi-serious rebellion which almost *any* kind of formal education will arouse in schoolchildren of any spirit; a rather more substantial part can be attributed to the hangover which the subject is still trying to shake off from its old indoctrinatory days of scriptural instruction (something which is made no easier by the anachronism of its mandatory status coupled with the often cynical doublethink which shores up its statutory nature with protestations of support, whilst whipping the carpet out from under the feet of the actual *practice* of the subject by providing the most minimal resources to carry it out). But although religious education *is* undoubtedly something of a special case, in terms of the negative feelings it tends to foster in pupils, the common rejection of the subject as pointless, as useless, as wholly without value because it has no practical end result, because it has nothing to do with securing a job, is surely symptomatic of a wider educational malaise, which may soon reach epidemic proportions and spread right across the curriculum unless something is done to counteract it.

Faced with a rejection of the subject as useless, the religious education teacher can adopt three basic strategies. The options they suggest are, I think, applicable to education in general, not just to one particular subject area. Thus in a climate where education as a whole is increasingly being perceived as valueless, it is perhaps timely to consider the three responses to this dilemma which are suggested by the experience of religious education. There is, of course, a fourth strategy too—simply giving up. There are many ways of doing this, from mindlessly following a set programme of work, designed to keep pupils occupied rather than teach them, to following no programme of work at all. Obviously there is no *educational* justification for adopting such a course of action, but in human terms of personal survival there may, on occasion, be something to recommend it. However, since this is very much a strategy of defeat, I shall not look at it here.

(1) The first strategy is simply to deny that religious education has no practical, vocational use. Thus the Christian Education Movement (CEM) and the Association of Teachers of Religious Education in Scotland (ATRES) have both produced leaflets entitled *The Career Value of Religious Education*.[2] These publications are at pains to point out that you don't have to be religious in order to take this subject, nor does it only point one in the direction of

a career in the church. They list a wide variety of jobs which a religious education qualification might lead to and remind readers that the vast majority of employers now view Religious Studies as a valid exam qualification. Journalism, social work, retailing, nursing and librarianship are just some of the professions listed as possibilities which may be open to people with a qualification in this area. Boots, Marks & Spencer, Heinz, insurance companies and banks are among the names of major employers listed who are happy to accept religious education in the same way that they accept other subjects in the broad area of the humanities. The CEM version of the leaflet also contains a directory listing details of first degree religion courses at 76 institutions in the UK, together with short interviews with graduates in Religious Studies and Theology who have found their way into retailing, stockbroking, publishing and so on.

Obviously it is important to make sure that pupils think ahead and that they are properly informed about the career implications of their subject choices. Especially in a subject like religious education, where many people are still surprised to find that there *are* exams, degree courses and employment possibilities, the efforts of CEM and ATRES are to be applauded (and one hopes that these publications will find a place in the careers rooms of every school in the country). And yet if we pursue this strategy of underlining the career value of a subject too far, it runs the risk of giving credence to the equation which states that education = qualifications = employment.

(2)   The second corrective strategy involves tackling the brick wall of rejection head-on. By making classes relevant and interesting, such a strategy seeks to contradict by classroom experience the point of view which dismisses the subject (or education in general) as pointless. The importance of religion in politics and current affairs, its role as a formative force in history and the way in which it addresses basic questions which confront everyone, means that religious education is fortunate enough to be dealing with subject matter which lends itself easily to such an endeavour. So long as we keep the right side of that rather blurred line which runs somewhere between education and entertainment, such a strategy is to be recommended—indeed it ought to be part and parcel of any good teacher's *modus operandi*. However, on its own I do not think that such a strategy is sufficient to rescue either religious education or education itself from the devaluation which they seem now so often to be faced with. If something has already been judged as pointless, it will take something more to break

through that evaluation than a straightforward counter-instance. Prejudice is notoriously blind to anything that does not fit in with its blinkered worldview and rock-solid preconceptions.

(3) The third strategy is to try to explain *why* religious education/education in general is intrinsically important, quite regardless of any career outcome. Such as a strategy applied in religious education does not assume that the value of learning about religion will be self-evident, nor is it a neutral approach in the sense of eschewing all expression of value judgment. On the contrary, it is a firmly evangelical endeavour (in a strictly educational sense), dedicated *not* to favouring any particular religious point of view but to advocating as unnegotiable the importance and value of becoming educated about this particular area of human experience.

If education about education is to be an effective counter to the deadweight of devaluation currently amassing within society at large, it would seem to require a carefully balanced blend of each of these three strategies. It seems to me, though, that it is the third strategy which needs greatest emphasis at the moment. If any real sense of purpose is to be (re)attached to the advancements in learning attempted at school and university, I think there is a definite need to preface and accompany even the most job-orientated course, even the most enthralling teaching, with a plainly stated and re-stated theoretical basis which leaves no one in any doubt of the immense value of spending time in this way.

'Theoretical' is not a word guaranteed to appeal to teachers, who are often understandably dismissive of the muddled abstractions which seem to play so central a role in the vocabulary of certain 'experts' who talk down to those at the chalk-face and which play no discernible role in the down-to-earth dynamics of the classroom. The theoretical foundation which education about education seeks to lay down, however, is designed to be covered over and built on, rather than to obtrude at odd and useless angles from the structures of learning. Its ethos is simple in the extreme: to demonstrate effectively for all to see that building such structures is vitally important; that what the teacher is doing, what the student is doing, what schools and colleges and universities stand for, is of crucial importance to the well-being of a civilized society, and that the education they offer has a far more extensive and valuable remit than merely to prepare people for employment. Alas, in the current political *zeitgeist* where, in terms of the somewhat crass economic touchstones now in use, education is a poor relation in comparison to so many other areas of endeavour (which of course depend on it), making such a point effectively will be far from easy.

Education about education seems to be missed out of many programmes of learning. Certainly in my own education I can think of no occasion when the value of the process I was undergoing was actually discussed. Yet in the same way that learning fire drill can be a somewhat pointless endeavour unless one is also made aware of the dangers of fire, so education without a reflexive element, without education about education itself, seems likewise to risk the absence of any undergirding sense of purpose for the whole endeavour. The dangers of fire and the dangers of ignorance are not altogether unlike—although the latter surely has vastly more destructive potential.

In view of this country's enormous investment in genocidal weaponry, it is worth remembering that the philosophy of defence rests on the supposition that we have a way of life which is *worth* protecting. High on the list of qualities usually associated with that highly valued way of life are freedom of speech and democracy. But unless education is properly valued (and treated—and funded— accordingly) it seems unlikely either that we will have much to say that is worth saying, or that the electorate will be such as to grace whatever government it happens to elect with the name 'democracy'. The implications of allowing the devaluation of education to continue are disturbingly wide-ranging and serious. How ironic it would be to take arms to defend a way of life that was spiritually bankrupt!

'*Education is valuable, regardless of its economic outcome*', is surely a thesis which every pupil should know how to prove as thoroughly as they learn what to do when a fire alarm sounds. It ought to be as basic to their knowledge as the ability to spell simple words or to realize that $2 + 2 = 4$. Such fundamental equations, as Tolstoy reminds us, continue to hold true even in the valley of the shadow of death. Education about education in general, and education about religious education in particular, is surely an important part of the set of precautions now needed if, as a society, we are to take no further steps towards so dark and terminal a destination.

One might have hoped that at this stage in British education there would no longer be any real need to demonstrate the import- ance of religious education. For surely it must be clear by now, to anyone who bothers to think about it, that the subject forms an integral (if not integrating) part of any balanced curriculum. Have there not been enough reports and committees and public debates for anyone who takes note of such things to be able to realize that religious education is—*indisputably*—an educationally valuable and viable subject? Its importance has been stated and re-stated, strategies for its implementation in the classroom have been drawn up, discussed and approved. At this stage what we need are the personnel and resources to translate words into effective action. Alas, there often seems to be little real political will to make this area a priority.

Academics can extol the worth of the subject, committees can echo their abstract assessments with more concrete propo-sals for classroom procedure, parents may voice their support, pupils express their interest, politicians may occasionally chime in and express their belief that religious education is important. But without the funds and facilities to train and appoint special-ist religious education teachers, such verbal pronouncements have very little real meaning in terms of what actually happens in the classroom.

The year 1984 saw the publication of two interesting, if depressing, reports: *Religious Education 11–18 in Wales*, pub-lished by the Welsh National Centre for Religious Education, and *Religious Education Provision 1984 for England and Wales* published by the Religious Education Council of England and Wales.[3] The Welsh survey showed religious education to be in a dismal state there, with pupils being taught the subject by over-worked and under-resourced teachers, a high percentage of whom had no adequate religious education qualification. The situation in England was also far from ideal. In fact the report on religious education provision, which contains a detailed statistical analysis of the situation, led to the Religious Education Council for Eng-land and Wales issuing 'suggestions for a campaign letter', which all those who were concerned about the subject were urged to send to their MPs and others in positions of authority. The following suggested paragraph was included in a list of points for possible inclusion in such a letter:

> The most serious crisis facing religious education is the shortage of specialist religious education teachers entering the profession. It is estimated that in 1985 there is an immediate need of between 2,000–7,000 specialist religious education teachers in secondary schools alone. The number of religious education specialists in training is 350.[4]

It would be nice to think that in Scotland and Northern Ireland the situation might be totally different, or that in the last five years things have changed significantly for the better. There are few signs that such optimism would be warranted. Thus in its *Supply of Teachers for the 1990s*, the Religious Education Council suggests that, quite apart from more longstanding difficulties, 'unless central initiative is taken to recruit and train more religious education specialists, the requirements of the 1988 Education Reform Act cannot be effectively met'.[5]

If the chairman of a national exam board suggested that between one third and a half of the country's secondary schools failed to meet the minimum standards for teaching English, maths or science, one might expect a public outcry. There would be surprise, denial, anger and demands for something to be done. When, as happened at the General Assembly of the Church of Scotland in 1989, the Chairman of the Scottish Exam Board suggested that this was precisely the situation with regard to religious education,[6] no one seemed particularly surprised or upset, and there has certainly been little sign of a storm of protest demanding that something should be done. What would be educationally unthinkable in almost any other area of the curriculum is, apparently, acceptable when it comes to this neglected subject. One suspects that the scandal of inadequate provision for religious education has been with us for so long that it has almost become invisible. Would it be any exaggeration to call the state of religious education in the UK a national disgrace?

As the then Education Secretary, Mr Kenneth Baker, stated in his inaugural IBM Lecture at the Royal Society, 'The central issue we have to tackle is the need to get the right number of teachers of quality.'[7] This would certainly seem to be the nub of the problem with regard to religious education. Genuine concern for religious education would be bound to result in an increase of funding to university departments of religious studies and theology (this is, after all, where fledgeling teachers acquire their specialist knowledge), to colleges of education (where they receive their professional training), and to the schools which are at present without adequate religious education staff. There is little evidence for such concern in Britain today. Instead, the focus of what political interest there is seems to be on religious instruction and religious observance, which are of course quite different from religious education. Unless government ministers responsible are ready to listen seriously to expert professional advice, not just to sectarian voices which see the subject as a vehicle for promoting their own point of view; unless they are prepared to take religion seriously as an important aspect of human life which education must explore, rather than as a set of particular doctrines which it must protect and propagate; unless they genuinely intend to do something to improve staffing levels in the subject, then there are surely grounds for fearing that the interest they intermittently voice for religious education is unlikely to achieve anything very constructive.

It is sometimes hard to distinguish between being reasonable and being unrealistic. Like the bee and the hoverfly they may have a similar appearance, with what is unrealistic sometimes taking on the protective colouring of its honey-producing, sting-bearing counterpart. Many purportedly educational proposals are, if we look at them carefully, somewhat unrealistic, advancing unnecessary or downright silly proposals under the guise of reason. They can be duly squashed without anyone being left much the wiser or more foolish; all that will suffer is the enthusiasm which bred them in the first place and enthusiasm is a naturally resilient resource. It seems to me, though, that many of those who are now dictating the course which education will follow in this country, have arrived at a point where they cannot tell the reasonable demand from the unreasonable proposal—or, if they can, that they do not much care. Trying to ensure the proper provision of religious education seems to me to be entirely, *compellingly*, reasonable, rather than constituting some sort of unrealistic claim on educational resources which ought indeed to be ignored. It is surely time that those who seek to swat the subject as carelessly as if it were some distracting fly buzzing in the ear of economics were alerted to the fact that bees and hover-flies are not the same. *Their* education is a matter of some urgency since the insect in question, if we allow them to strike it down, may, in the end, turn out to have a socially fatal sting.

Notes

1   H G Wells, *The Outline of History, Being a Plain History of Life and Mankind*, London: 1951, p1192.

2   Copies of the Christian Education Movement's *The Career Value of Religious Education* are available from: RE Today, 47 Prospect Place, Exeter, EX4 6NA.

3   Religious Education Council for England and Wales, *Religious Education Provision 1984* (the Council may be contacted via the Religious Education Enquiry Centre at St Martin's College, Lancaster, LA1 3JD). Welsh National Centre for Religious Education, *Religious Education 11–18 in Wales* (1984) (the Centre may be contacted at

School of Education, University College of North Wales, St Mary's, Lôn Pobty, Bangor, Gwynedd).

4   'Suggestions for a Campaign Letter' accompanying *Religious Education Provision 1984*.

5   The Religious Education Council of England and Wales, *Supply of Teachers for 1990s*.

6   Reported in the *Times Educational Supplement*, 2 June 1989.

7   Reported in the *Times Educational Supplement*, 26 May 1989.

Acknowledgments

Much of this book has appeared in article form in the *Times Educational Supplement Scotland* (now renamed the *Times Scottish Education Supplement*). I am grateful to its editor for allowing so much of my work on religious education to find space in the pages of his paper over the last five years, and for permission to reprint it here. Thanks are also due to the *TSES's* sister publication south of the border, the *Times Educational Supplement*, where some short sections of *Biting the Bullet* have appeared.

In addition, I am grateful to the editors of the following journals, in which portions of this book found their first published form: the *British Journal of Religious Education*, the *Farmington Institute Occasional Papers* series, the *Media Education Journal*, the *Month* and the *Times Higher Education Supplement*.

Bibliography

Writing in 1759, Dr Johnson identified 'the multiplication of books' as 'one of the peculiarities which distinguish the present age'. He went on to speculate whether, just as a surfeit of laws can often characterize a corrupt society, so an ignorant one might be marked by having many books. One wonders what moral he would have drawn from the enormous proliferation of book production which has taken place in the 230 years since he wrote. Almost every field of study has been affected, and religious education is no exception. It is rather doubtful, however, if some of the published material now available would pass Johnson's criteria of usefulness! Having, in *Biting the Bullet*, made my own small contribution to the burgeoning literature on the subject, I do not want to compound matters by burdening the reader with a comprehensive bibliography. These are not difficult to find (or, in this age of computer searches, to assemble for oneself). Instead, I want merely to list a *selection* of material which I have found useful. My emphasis is on journals and collections of papers, since I think that the best work in this area still finds expression in article, rather than book, form.

(a) Journals

British Journal of Religious Education (The main professional Journal on the British scene. Published quarterly and available from: The Christian Education Movement, Lancaster House, Borough Road, Isleworth, Middlesex TW7 5DU).

Farmington Institute Occasional Papers (These discussion papers cover a wide range of concerns within religious education. Available from: The Farmington Institute for Christian Studies, 4 Park Town, Oxford OX2 6SH).

Religious Education (An important academic journal which, though American in emphasis, contains much material of general interest to anyone working in this field. It is inter-faith in outlook, publishing articles from members of many different religious viewpoints. Published quarterly and available from: Editorial Offices, Box 2025, Virginia Commonwealth University, Richmond, VA 23284-2025. *Religious Education* is the journal of the Religious Education Association of the United States and Canada, and the Association of Professors and Researchers in Religious Education.)

Shap Mailing (The Shap Working Party on World Religions in Education took its name from the village of Shap in the Lake District where the movement started after a conference in 1969. The Working Party's annual mailings, which include the very useful *Calendar of Religious Festivals*, cover a wide range of themes. Topics have included: Women in Religion (1988); Religions in Britain (1986); Worship in World Faiths (1985); Pilgrimage (1983). Details from: West Sussex Institute of Higher Education, Bishop Otter College, Chichester).

Times Educational Supplement and *Times Scottish Education Supplement* (These weekly publications carry occasional articles on religious education. Every year, usually in December, there is at least one special Religious Education Supplement).

(b) Books

Cole, Owen (ed), *World Faiths in Education*, London: Unwin Education Books, 1978.

Fowler, James W, *Stages of Faith, the Psychology of Human Development and the Quest for Meaning*, San Francisco: Harper & Row, 1980.

Goldman, Ronald, *Readiness for Religion, a Basis for Developmental Religious Education*, London: Routledge & Kegan Paul, 1965.

Hull, John (ed), *New Directions in Religious Education*, Lewes: Falmer Press, 1982.

Hull, John, *Studies in Religion and Education*, Lewes: Falmer Press, 1984.

Hulmes, Edward, *Commitment and Neutrality in Religious Education*, London: Geoffrey Chapman (Cassell), 1979.

Smart, Ninian, *Secular Education and the Logic of Religion*, London: Faber & Faber, 1968.

Smart, Ninian & Donald Horder (eds), *New Movements in Religious Education*, London: Temple Smith, 1975.

(c)   Reference

Sutcliffe, John (ed), *A Dictionary of Religious Education*, London: SCM, 1984.

Subject Index

In order to keep the index within manageable bounds, no attempt has been made to index religious education or the various world religions to which reference has been made.

Name Index

Notes

Notes

Notes

Notes

Notes

Notes

Notes

Notes

Notes

Notes